The Thousand Names of
Shiva

VIJAYA KUMAR

A Sterling Paperbacks

STERLING PAPERBACKS
An imprint of
Sterling Publishers (P) Ltd.
A-59 Okhla Industrial Area, Phase-II,
New Delhi-110020.
Tel: 26387070, 26386209; Fax: 91-11-26383788
E-mail: ghai@nde.vsnl.net.in
www.sterlingpublishers.com

The Thousand Names of Shiva
Copyright © 2006 by Sterling Publishers Pvt. Ltd.
ISBN 81 207 3008 9

Published by Sterling Publishers Pvt. Ltd., New Delhi-110 020.
Printed at Sterling Publishers Pvt. Ltd., New Delhi-110020.

Preface

Sahasranama or the thousand names of the most extensive elaboration of the Divin most popular and the holiest form of the Di

Every name or *stotra* of the Divine Being is of a particular cult deity, like Vishnu, Shiva, G so on. These names, strung together into verses, inexhaustibility of the attributes and glories of that glories of God manifest themselves in many way the sentient and the insentient, and by chanting th the devotees show their adoration for the Lord. T create the holy link with their Maker.

The thousand names of Shiva were first cha Krishna for the benefit of Yudhishthira in the presence of Bhishma. Then came the thousand names of Vishnu by Bhishma to Yudhishthira in Krishna's presence on the same occasion. Since Ganesha is the Lord of all obstacles, and is the one whose worship is foremost, his thousand names came into being.

Each of these books need not necessarily contain exactly thousand names. The numbers may be increased or decreased according to the devotee's choice. What matters ultimately is that these names are the shortest expressions of the profoundest meanings.

Preface

1. Sthira: *Firm And Steadfast*

ॐ स्थिराय नमः

Representing the union of substance and energy, Lord Shiva is firm and steadfast unlike Shakti, his other half, who is transient.

2. Sthanu: *The Pillar*

ॐ स्थानवे नमः

Symbolising the firmness and solidity of a rock, Lord Shiva is the pillar supporting the universe.

3. Prabhu: *The Lord Of All*

ॐ प्रभावे नमः

Representing the cyclic process of generation, destruction and regeneration, Lord Shiva is the Lord of all.

4. Bheema: *The Terrible*

ॐ भीमाय नमः

He is the Roaring God, the terrible One, who, if angry, can destroy everything, but, if pleased, can be kind and beneficent.

5. Pravara: *Par Excellence*

ॐ प्रवराय नमः

He personifies all that is intelligent and perfect, and is beyond comparison, for He is the Supreme One.

6. Varada: *The Bestower Of Boons*

ॐ वरदाय नमः

As the most Benign Deity, Lord Shiva is capable of bestowing even the impossible boons. He is pleased with sincere and genuine devotion, because for him, the spirit is more important than the form.

7. Vara: *The Ultimate*

ॐ वराय नमः

Having the Ultimate Reality, He is the Omniscient, the Omnipresent and Lord Supreme.

8. Sarvatma: *The Self In All Beings*

ॐ सर्वात्मने नमः

Lord Shiva, the Light of all lighted manifestation, dwells in every being. Realise this Self to attain salvation.

9. Sarvavikhyata: *The Core Of All Beings*

ॐ सर्वविरव्याताय नमः

He dwelling in the core of all beings, stands rock-like and majestically in the centre of the universe, symbolising the beacon light that draws everything to it.

10. Sarva: *The All-in-all*

ॐ सर्वस्मै नमः

He is the Protector of all beings, the Destroyer of evil, the Ultimate Reality who is the root cause for all change, though Himself remaining changeless.

11. Sarvakara: *The Doer Of All*

ॐ सर्वकराय नमः

He is the Creator, the Universal Builder, the Divine Master Craftsman who has designed all creation.

12. Bhava: *The Existence*

ॐ भवाय नमः

He is the Source of all light, through whom all else is illuminated, and the source of all existence.

13. Jati: *The One With Matted Hair*

ॐ जटिने नमः

His flowing tendrils, matted hair symbolise Him as the Lord of wind, Vayu, who is the subtle form of breath all around.

14. Charmi: *Attired In Animal Skin*

ॐ चर्मिने नमः

Lord Shiva, in the scanty clothings of animal skins, indicates the necessity of rising above body consciousness.

15. Shikhandi: *Tufted Hair Like Peacock's Crest*

ॐ शिखण्डीने नमः

With spirally braided tuft, resembling a peacock's crest, He shines like gold.

16. Sarvanga: *He Who Has The Universe As His Limb*

ॐ सर्वांगाय नमः

He who manifests and transcends the mundane has the entire universe as His limb.

17. Sarvabhavana: *One Who Manifests And Maintains All*

ॐ सर्वभावनाय नमः

Lord Shiva, the Divine, manifests, putting on the appearance of the mundane, to sustain and maintain all.

18. Hara: *The Withholder*

ॐ हराय नमः

He alone manifests Himself and apart from Him, nothing exists. Projecting the universe, maintaining it and withholding it is His *maya*

19. Harinaksha: *The Deer-eyed*

ॐ हरिनाक्षाय नमः

Like the soft-eyed deer, there is grace in his gaze.

20. Sarvabhootahara: *The Destroyer of Creation*

ॐ सर्वभूतहराय नमः

Lord Shiva, who destroys, causes things to assume new phases of existence, and hence, even as He destroys, He creates.

21. Prabhu: *The Enjoyer*

ॐ प्रभवे नमः

Lord Shiva, the Bright or Happy One, who is the most bountiful of the gods, as Conscience records all enjoyments.

22. Pravruthi: *Manifestation*

ॐ श्री प्रवृत्तये नमः

He posits Himself at all levels as all beings. Man should adore all that he senses as the manifestations of Shiva.

23. Nivruthi: *The Original State*

ॐ निवृत्तये नमः

He destroys all that He creates, and regenerates, tracing back to the original state.

24. Niyata: *The Self-controlled*

ॐ नियताय नमः

Being the Supreme Controller of the five senses, He regains His original state by controlling the senses.

25. Shashvata: *The Eternal*

ॐ शाश्वताय नमः

He is the Supreme God that ever was, and ever will be, without beginning or end.

26. Dhruva: *The Immovable*

ॐ ध्रुवाये नमः

Lord Shiva, the very cause of the being of this world, is the Immovable and the Immutable.

27. Shmashanavasi: *The Dweller Of The Cremation Ground*

ॐ श्मशानवासिने नमः

The cremation ground is his favourite residence of Lord Shiva, suggesting that He stands for the transcendence of the mundane.

28. Bhagavan: *The Possessor Of The Six Graces*

ॐ भगवते नमः

Lord Shiva, the Supreme Deity, is the master of the six graces — wisdom, beauty, fame, renunciation, lordship and heroism.

29. Khachara: *The Space-dweller*

ॐ खचराय नमः

Lord Shiva, who alone is the Persisting Reality, dwells in the space of each heart, denoting that the inner space in the heart transcends the phenomenon.

30. Gochara: *The Perceiver Through The Senses*

ॐ गोचराय नमः

Being the inner Controller of the organs, He can be sensed or perceived only through the five senses.

31. Ardana: *The Punisher*

ॐ अर्दनाय नमः

When one violates or abuses the senses, retribution or punishment comes in the form of torment.

32. Abhivadhya: *Worshipped By All*

ॐ अभिवाद्याय नमः

Lord Shiva, the Craftsman deft in weaving illusions, is involuntarily worshipped by all.

33. Mahakarma: *The Great Act*

ॐ महाकर्मणे नमः

He is the Performer of the great act of creation, preservation and destruction of the universe.

34. Tapasvi: *The Ascetic*

ॐ तपस्विने नमः

The mind, which is constantly in a state of flux, has to be subdued, and the ascetic, by channelling his mind to the spiritual can transcend all that is material.

35. Bhootabhavana: *The Creator Of The Five Elements*

ॐ भूतभावनाय नमः

Lord Shiva, the Divine, who creates and dissolves the world at will, is the Creator of the five elements — air, water, earth, fire and ether.

9

36. Unmataveshaprachhanna: *Concealed In The Guise Of Madness*

ॐ उन्मत्तवेप्रच्छन्नाय नमः

Lord Shiva, universally and involuntarily worshipped, is actually mad after devotees.

37. Sarvalokaprajapati: *The Lord Of All Existence*

ॐ सर्वलोकप्रजापतये नमः

He is the Lord of all existence, through whom the entire world is created, and ultimately coalesces with Him only.

38. Maharoopa: *All-round Form*

ॐ महारूपाय नमः

He is the Great Atman, pervading all in all forms, but stationed in the single syllable 'Aum'.

39. Mahakaya: *The Cosmic Body*

ॐ महाकायाय नमः

The attributeless and illusory Lord Shiva has the universe as His body.

40. Vrusharoopa: *In The Form Of The Bull*

ॐ वृषरूपाय नमः

He is where *Dharma* prevails, and the bull is the personification of *Dharma*.

41. Mahayasha: *The Famous*

ॐ महायशसे नमः

Lord Shiva, who is the most bountiful of the gods, and is the Indispensable One, becomes the Famous.

42. Mahatma: *The Great-minded*

ॐ महात्मने नमः

He is the embodiment of the bliss that accrues by gaining knowledge.

43. Sarvabhootatma: *The Self Of All Beings*

ॐ सर्वभूतात्मने नमः

He dwells in all beings. Realise this Self to attain Him.

44. Vishwaroopa: *The Universal Form*

ॐ विश्वरूपाय नमः

Lord Shiva, the Manifest and the Unmanifest, has the universe as His form.

45. Mahahanu: *The Great Jaws*

ॐ महाहनवे नमः

Lord Shiva, the All-Powerful Supreme Lord, is capable of swallowing the universe.

46. Lokapala: *The Ruler Of The Worlds*

ॐ लोकपालाय नमः

As the Ruler of the three worlds, He is the Omniscient and the Omnipotent.

47. Antarhitatma: *The Concealed Self*

ॐ अन्तर्हितात्मने नमः

He dwells concealed in each being, and the egoists think of the non-self as Self.

48. Prasada: *Clearness*

ॐ प्रसादाय नमः

Lord Shiva, the Personification of bliss, is established in clear, blissful serenity.

49. Hayagardabhi: *Riding The Mule-driven Chariot*

ॐ श्री हयगर्दभये नमः

Though Nandi, the bull, is His vehicle, yet He also rides the mule-driven chariot, denoting mastery over obstinacy.

50. Pavitra: *The Purifier*

ॐ पवित्राय नमः

Lord Shiva, personifying auspiciousness, protects the Self from the mundane.

51. Mahan: *The Worshipful*

ॐ महते नमः

Being the favourite of His devotees, He is worshipped with great respect and adoration.

52. Niyama: *The Ordinance*

ॐ नियमाय नमः

He desires from His devotees purity, self-surrender, self-composure, frankness and spiritual study.

53. Niyamashrita: *Attained Though The Ordinance*

ॐ नियमाश्रिताय नमः

By transcending one's ego, man can attain to the Lord, for then the means and the goals become the same.

54. Sarvakarma: *All Activities Are His*

ॐ सर्वकर्मणे नमः

He is the Great Performer, and nothing moves in the universe without His will.

55. Swayambhoota: *Self-manifestation*

ॐ स्वयंभूताय नमः

Veiled by His divine *Maya*, He is not revealed to all. His self-manifestation is illusory.

56. Adi: *The Very First*

ॐ आद्ये नमः

Lord of the past, the present and the future, He is the Very First, having no beginning or end.

57. Adikara: *The Creator Of Brahma*

ॐ आदिकराय नमः

When He pervaded all space, being desirous of creation. He created a bubble from whence emerged Brahma.

58. Nidhi: *The Treasure*

ॐ निधये नमः

He represents all the treasures in the universe, including the *Padma nidhi* and the *Shanka nidhi*.

59. Sahastraksha: *Omni-eyed*

ॐ सहस्त्राक्षाय नमः

Lord Shiva, with His three eyes, the frontal eye being the one of higher perception, perceives through all the eyes of all beings.

60. Vishalaksha: *The Universal Seer*

ॐ विशालाक्षाय नमः

Lord Shiva, with His vertical third eye in the middle of His forehead, has extreme visionary power.

61. Soma: *The Spouse Of Uma*

ॐ सोमाय नमः

He is the consort of Uma, the ever-graceful daughter of the lofty mountains.

62. Nakshatrasadaka: *The Benefactor Of The Stars*

ॐ नक्षत्रसादकाय नमः

He is the Source of all light through whom all else is illuminated.

63. Chandra: *The Moon*

ॐ चन्द्राय नमः

Like the waning and waxing moon, He procreates and destroys.

64. Surya: *The Sun*

ॐ सूर्याय नमः

With the brilliance of a thousand suns, He shines radiantly.

65. Shani: *Saturn*

ॐ शनये नमः

Saturn has malefic effects, and Lord Shiva destroys all that is malefic, and is malefic towards violators of the Dharma.

66. Ketu: *Descending Node*

ॐ केतवे नमः

Lord Shiva, the Controller of all planets, is Ketu in one of His manifestations.

67. Graha: *Rahu*

ॐ ग्रहाय नमः

As the Supreme Lord of the planets, He created Rahu who obscures the sun and moon.

68. Grahapati: *Mars*

ॐ ग्रहपतये नमः

As Creator of the planets, He like Mars, can be troublesome to those who do not worship Him.

69. Vara: *The Worshipful*

ॐ वराय नमः

Among the planets created by Him, Brihaspati (Jupiter) is the most revered and worshipped.

70. Atri: *Mercury (Budha)*

ॐ अत्रये नमः

Denoting auspiciousness, Mercury, ruled by Lord Shiva, is beneficent.

71. Atryanamaskarta: *Pays Homage To Wife Of Atri*

ॐ अत्र्यानमस्कर्त्रे नमः

He paid homage to Anusuya, the wife of Atri, for giving birth to Dattratreya and Durvasa, two illustrious sons.

72. Mrugabanarpana: *He Who Aimed An Arrow At The Stag*

ॐ मृगबाणार्पणाय नमः

When the ritualistic sages produced a stag by white magic, He aimed an arrow at it and possessed it.

73. Anagha: *The Sinless*

ॐ अनघाय नमः

He is faultless and pure. The destruction of the sacrificial fire did not taint Him as He is sinless.

74. Mahatapa: *Extremely Austere*

ॐ महातपसे नमः

He is the last word in austerity, penance and meditation.

75. Ghoratapa: *Terrible Austerity*

ॐ घोरतपसे नमः

Lord Shiva, the perfect and greatest ascetic, is totally immersed in His Spiritual Excellence.

76. Adeena: *Exalted But Humble*

ॐ अदिनाय नमः

Though He appears condescending and frightful, yet, He is the most humble and bountiful.

77. Deenasadhaka: *Uplifter Of The Poor*

ॐ दीनसाधकाय नमः

Being very fond of His devotees, He transforms the insignificant into the great.

78. Samvatsarakara: *The Creator Of Time*

ॐ संवत्सरकराय नमः

He represents Time, endless and inexorable. The past, present and future are fragment of One Time, merging in Him.

79. Mantra: *The Mystic Sound*

ॐ मन्त्राय नमः

He is the Originator of the mystic sound 'Aum', and chanting this repeatedly strengthens the mind.

80. Pramanam: *The Evidence*

ॐ प्रमाणाय नमः

Lord Shiva, the Manifest and Unmanifest, is self-existent.

81. Paramayatapa: *Extremely Austere*

ॐ परमायतपसे नमः

Lord Shiva, a Supreme Ascetic clothed in austerity, can be attained and realised only through penance and the senses.

82. Yogi: *The Great Ascetic*

ॐ योगिने नमः

He teaches mankind to mortify the body and suppress emotions and passions, so as to reach Him.

83. Yojya: *Worthy Of Union*

ॐ योज्याय नमः

He is the Great Spirit in whom one would want to merge oneself.

84. Mahabeeja: *The Great Seed*

ॐ महाबीजाय नमः

He is the Divine Source of everything.

85. Mahareta: *The Great Reflection*

ॐ महारेतसे नमः

Lord Shiva, dwelling in every being, reflects Himself as the Self.

86. Mahabala: *The Great Strength*

ॐ महाबलाय नमः

The invincible Lord Shiva is the Great Lord of divine power and strength.

87. Suvarnareta: *The Golden Semen*

ॐ सुवर्णरेतसे नमः

Being the Supreme Ascetic, His *retas* (semen) assumed the brilliance of a thousand suns.

88. Sarvajna: *The Omniscient*

ॐ सर्वज्ञाय नमः

Known for His Supreme wisdom, there is nothing beyond His knowledge.

89. Subeeja: *The Best Seed*

ॐ सुबीजाय नमः

Lord Shiva, the source of everything, remains constant and unchanging.

90. Beejavahana: *The Seed-bearer*

ॐ बीजवाहनाय नमः

His vehicle is the seed of nescience.

91. Dashabahu: *Ten-armed*

ॐ दशबाहवे नमः

Being the embodiment of Eternal Time, Lord Shiva, with His ten arms and five faces, is invincible and eternal.

92. Animisha: *Awake And Alert*

ॐ अनिमिषाय नमः

He is the Divine watchman who never sleeps, and is ever alert.

93. Neelakantha: *Blue-necked*

ॐ नीलकण्ठाय नमः

He partakes of the poison produced by beings to save them.

94. Umapati: *Consort of Uma*

ॐ उमापतये नमः

Lord Shiva and Uma form the Eternal Couple who are inseparable.

95. Vishwaroopa: *The Cosmic Form*

ॐ विश्वरूपाय नमः

Devotees see Him in various forms, but His cosmic form can be perceived only through the senses.

96. Swayamshreshtta: *Innately Excellent*

ॐ स्वयंश्रेष्ठाय नमः

He is Knowledge, Great Intellect and Bliss, par excellence.

97. Balaveera: *The Mighty*

ॐ बलवीराय नमः

Embodying divine power and strength, He is beyond birth and death.

17

98. Abalogana: *The Inert Group*

ॐ अबलोगणाय नमः

Understanding the twenty-four categories of the Sankhya, enlightens man in regard to the cosmos and his own place in it.

99. Ganakarta: *The Creator Of The Categories*

ॐ गणकर्त्रे नमः

He created the categories of the Sankhya darshana for man to realise Him.

100. Ganapati: *The Lord Of The Categories*

ॐ गणपतये नमः

Lord Shiva, having created the twenty-four categories of the Sankhya, is their Lord.

101. Digvasa: *Clothed In Space*

ॐ दिग्वाससे नमः

Lord Shiva, who has the universe as His body, is clothed in space.

102. Kama: *Lust*

ॐ कामाय नमः

Lord Shiva, the Controller of the five senses, conquers all and quells the agitated and lustful mind.

103. Mantravid: *Well-versed In Mantra*

ॐ मन्त्रविदे नमः

Lord Shiva, the Originator of the sound 'Aum', is a great fount and storehouse of limitless knowledge, being well-versed in the mantra.

104. Paramomantra: *The Supreme Mantra*

ॐ परमाया मन्त्राय नमः

By chanting the central mantra 'Om nama shivaya' repeatedly, one can hope to seek His divine blessings.

105. Sarvabhavakara: *The Creator Of Existence*

ॐ सर्वभावकराय नमः

Lord Shiva, through whom the whole universe is instinct, is the Ultimate Power responsible for existence.

106. Hara: *The Attractor*

ॐ हराय नमः

Just as flowers attract bees, Lord Shiva attracts His devotees.

107. Kamandaludhara: *The Holder Of The Mendicant's Bowl*

ॐ कमण्डलुधराय नमः

Lord Shiva, the Great Ascetic that He is, holds a mendicant's bowl, symbolising renunciation.

108. Dhanvi: *The Bowman*

ॐ धन्विने नमः

He wields the bow made of Mount Sumeru, and its low-strings, of Lord Vasuki the snake, while the fiery arrow is graced by Lord Vishnu.

109. Banahasta: *The Archer*

ॐ बाणहस्ताय नमः

Just as the quick arrow from an archer's bow whizzes past in a flash, so are all things material of little and fleeting consequence.

110. Kapalvan: *The Skull-bearer*

ॐ कपालवते नमः

He wears a garland of skulls and ornaments of bones, signifying that something profane can become profound, leading to Self-awakening.

111. Ashani: *The Thunderbolt*

ॐ अशनये नमः

He wields the thunderbolt, destroying all egos and arrogance.

112. Shataghni: *The Hundred-killer*

ॐ शतघ्निने नमः

Lord Shiva, the Destroyer, wields the weapon called Shakti which is capable of total destruction.

113. Khadgi: *The Sword*

ॐ खड्गिने नमः

Holding the sword in His hand, He quells enemies, thus providing succour to the hapless.

114. Pattishi: *The Wielder Of The Battle-axe*

ॐ पट्टिशिने नमः

Lord Shiva, wielding the battle-axe, delights in destruction for its own sake.

115. Ayudhi: *Wielding the Trident*

ॐ आयुधिने नमः

He wields the trident, denoting that He combines in His Person the three attributes — of Creator-Destroyer-Regenerator.

116. Mahan: *The Adorable*

ॐ महते नमः

Lord Shiva, the Divine Absolute, is most adorable.

117. Sruvahasta: *With The Sacrificial Ladle In Hand*

ॐ सुवहस्ताय नमः

Lord Shiva, known for His austerities and learnings, holds the sacrificial ladle in His hand, signifying transcendence of mind over matter.

118. Suroopa: *The Beautiful*

ॐ सुरूपाय नमः

He looks enchanting and magnificent, seated on His mount Nandi.

119. Teja: *The Energetic*

ॐ तेजसे नमः

Lord Shiva, the Beacon of guidance, is full of vigour and divine energy.

120. Tejaskara Nidhi: *The Source Of Effulgence*

ॐ तेजस्करायनिधये नमः

Lord Shiva, being most bountiful, showers effulgence on His devotees.

121. Ushneeshi: *The Wearer Of Turban*

ॐ उष्णीषिने नमः

Lord Shiva, wearing the turban in one of His manifestations, is above all things superficial.

122. Suvaktra: *With Handsome Face*

ॐ सुवक्त्राय नमः

He looks handsome with a moon-like face, eyes shaped like the lotus and shining brilliantly, ears resplendent with earrings, and matted hair with tendrils softly kissing His forehead.

123. Udagra: *The Eminent*

ॐ उदग्राय नमः

He is of lofty fame, ever revered by great sages, gods and celestials.

124. Vinata: *The Modest*

ॐ विनताय नमः

Lord Shiva, though Supreme, who is beyond comparison, is modest.

125. Dheergha: *The Tallest*

ॐ दीर्घाय नमः

Lord Shiva, who is beyond measure, is the tallest.

126. Harikesha: *Aware Of The World*

ॐ हरिकेशाय नमः

Lord Shiva, the Controller of the senses, allows one to perceive the mundane world through the senses.

127. Suteertha: *The Holiest Preceptor*

ॐ सुतीर्थाय नमः

Lord Shiva, the Greatest Ascetic, is also the Holiest Preceptor.

128. Krishna: *Existence-Knowledge-Bliss*

ॐ कृष्णाय नमः

He is the True Being, the Conscious, the Perfect Bliss.

129. Shrugalarupa: *In The Form Of A Jackal*

ॐ श्रृगालरूपाय नमः

He assumed the form of a jackal to console a Brahmana insulted by a Vaishya.

130. Siddhartha: *The Achiever Of Everything*

ॐ सिद्धार्थाय नमः

Lord Shiva, who creates, destroys and recreates, achieves everything, leaving nothing to be achieved.

131. Munda: *The Shaven One*

ॐ मुण्डाय नमः

He as the Shaven One indicates that He is a Sannyasin.

132. Sarvashubhankara: *The Doer Of Good To All*

ॐ सर्वशुभंकराय नमः

Lord Shiva, the Performer of amazing deeds, is the Doer of good to all.

133. Aja: *The Unborn*

ॐ अजाय नमः

He is the Unborn, who has no beginning or end.

134. Bahurupa: *The Multi-Formed*

ॐ बहुरूपाय नमः

He is formless and yet with many forms for mankind.

135. Gandhadhari: *The Fragrance Bearer*

ॐ गन्धधारिने नमः

The symbol of perfection in the control of senses is fragrance.

136. Kapardi: *The Wearer Of Knotted Hair*

ॐ कपर्दिने नमः

Lord Shiva, bearing the heavenly Ganga in His matted hair, wears His hair in a knot.

22

137. Urdhvareta: *One Who Makes The Semen Flow*

ॐ ऊर्ध्वरेतसे नमः

This is a characteristic of a perfect celibate.

138. Urdhvalinga: *With An Upturned Phallus*

ॐ ऊर्ध्वलिंगाय नमः

One who is a novice in sexual pleasures is equated with Shiva, the Perfect Brahmachari.

139. Urdhvashayi: *Lying On One's Back Only*

ॐ ऊर्ध्वशायिने नमः

Shiva, the embodiment of perfection, lies on His back only, signifying He is beyond carnal pleasures.

140. Nabhastala: *The Space-dweller*

ॐ नभस्थलाय नमः

Lord Shiva, the all-pervasive, who is in unison with Shakti, dwells in every being.

141. Trijati: *With Three Matted Locks*

ॐ त्रिजटिने नमः

He wears three matted locks in a knot in which is concealed the heavenly Ganga.

142. Cheeravasa: *The Bark-wearer*

ॐ चीरवाससे नमः

He is clothed in the bark of trees, embodying the simplicity of an ascetic.

143. Rudra: *The Praiseworthy*

ॐ रुद्राय नमः

Lord Shiva, as Rudra, uplifts those in distress, thus earning their praises.

144. Senapati: *The Supreme Commander*

ॐ सेनापतये नमः

Lord Shiva, dwelling in the hearts of beings as Pure Consciousness, commands all virtuous people.

23

145. Vibhu: *The Omnipresent*

ॐ विभवे नमः

He is the Omnipresent, residing in every space and being.

146. Ahaschara: *The Mover In The Daytime*

ॐ अहश्चराय नमः

All beings moving about in the daytime, have their origin in Him.

147. Naktamchara: *The Mover At Night*

ॐ नक्तंचराय नमः

While the world sleeps at night, He moves about and keeps vigil.

148. Tigmamanyu: *Fiercely Wrathful*

ॐ तिग्ममन्यवे नमः

Lord Shiva, the personification of calmness and tenderness, exercises His wrath in the destruction of all that is evil.

149. Suvarchasa: *Effulgence*

ॐ सुवर्चसाय नमः

Being the manifestation of the sacred study and austerity, He dazzles in His brilliant glory.

150. Gajaha: *The Slayer Of The Elephant*

ॐ गजघ्ने नमः

He is the Slayer of the demon who, as an elephant, destroyed the city of Varanasi.

151. Daitya: *The Slayer Of The Daityas*

ॐ दैत्यघ्ने नमः

He is the Slayer of the demons who were destructive and evil.

152. Kala: *Time*

ॐ कालाय नमः

He represents Time, endless and inexorable.

153. Lokadhata: *The Lord Of The Three Worlds*

ॐ लोकधात्रे नमः

Lord Shiva, the Omniscient and Omnipresent, is the Lord of the three worlds that He created.

154. Gunakara: *The Storehouse Of Virtues*

ॐ गुणाकराय नमः

He is the Source of all virtuous things, and is the divine storehouse of these.

155. Simhashardoolarupa: *In The Lion-tiger Form*

ॐ सिंहशार्दूलरुपाय नमः

He manifests in various forms of ferocious animals, to vanquish all that is evil.

156. Ardracharmambaravruta: *Attired In An Elephant's Bloodstained Skin*

ॐ आर्द्रचर्माम्बरावृताय नमः

He is above all that is mundane, and attired in bloodstained skins, shows that He is Master of the senses.

157. Kalayogi: *The Yogi Who Transcends Time*

ॐ कालयोगिने नमः

Lord Shiva, the Greatest Yogi, transcends time — past, present and future, which are fragments of One Time merging in Him.

158. Mahanada: *The Great Sound*

ॐ महानादाय नमः

He is the Originator of the great sound 'Aum', and this cosmic sound is experienced in yoga-trance.

159. Sarvakama: *The Embodiment Of All Desires*

ॐ सर्वकामाय नमः

Being the Embodiment of all desires, He fulfils the desires of the devotees.

160. Chutushpatha: *The Four Paths*

ॐ चतुष्पथाय नमः

He is worshipped in four specific methods — Vishwa, Taijasa, Prajna and Shiva.

161. Nishachara: *The Night-walker*

ॐ निशाचराय नमः

Like the goblins, spirits, ghosts and sprites roaming around at night, He stalks the four corners of the universe, suggestive of rising above all that is material.

162. Pretachari: *The Companion Of The Dead*

ॐ प्रतचारिने नमः

The cemetery being His favourite ground, He is a constant companion of the dead.

163. Bhutachari: *The Companion Of The Goblin*

ॐ भूतचारिने नमः

Lord Shiva, who loves the burial ground, is attended by goblins who are His companions during such visits.

164. Maheswara: *The Great Lord*

ॐ महेश्वराय नमः

He is the Supreme Ruler, the Ultimate who is the pinnacle of devotion.

165. Bahubhuta: *The Many Forms*

ॐ बहुभूताय नमः

Lord Shiva, who is The One, becomes Many whenever He desires.

166. Bahudhara: *The Upholder Of The Many*

ॐ बहुधराय नमः

Lord Shiva, being most bountiful, is the Uplifter and Sustainer of the teeming existence.

167. Swarbhanu: *Rahu The Nescience*

ॐ स्वर्भानवे नमः

He is like Rahu, nescient and agnostic, as the situation demands.

168. Amita: *The Immeasurable*

ॐ अमिताय नमः

He is limitless, without measure or count.

169. Gati: *The Goal*

ॐ गतये नमः

He is the Divine Goal, which is the focus of all existence.

170. Nrityapriya: *The Delighter In Dance*

ॐ नृत्यप्रियाय नमः

He delights in the rhythmic movement of the cosmos, which is His dance.

171. Nityanarta: *The Eternal Dancer*

ॐ नित्यनर्ताय नमः

The universe, with its rhythmic movements, is the expression of the eternal dance of Lord Shiva.

172. Nartaka: *The Cause of Others' Dances*

ॐ नर्तकाय नमः

When He dances in delight, the entire creation follows suit.

173. Sarvalalasa: *The Friend Of All*

ॐ सर्वलालसाय नमः

He is Love, and is the friend of all.

174. Ghora: *The Terrible*

ॐ घोराय नमः

He combines the stormy with the pacific, thus invoking involuntary adulation.

175. Mahatapa: *The Great Ascetic*

ॐ महातपसे नमः

By His simplicity and austerity, the Great Ascetic, Lord Shiva, teaches mankind to rise above the material world.

176. Pasha: *The Noose*

ॐ पाशाय नमः

Holding the noose in His hand, He fosters beings in the process of evolution.

177. Nitya: *The Eternal*

ॐ नित्याय नमः

The indestructible Shiva is the Persisting Reality.

178. Giriruha: *The Dweller of The Mountain*

ॐ गिरिरुहाय नमः

He dwells on Mount Kailash, making it His abode, with Parvati beside Him.

179. Nabha: *The Sky*

ॐ नभसे नमः

Like the limitless expanse of the sky, He is pure and endless.

180. Sahasrahasta: *The Multi-armed*

ॐ सहस्त्रहस्ताय नमः

Lord Shiva, manifest in various forms, is multi-armed, wielding various weapons for punishing the evil-doers.

181. Vijaya: *The Victory*

ॐ विजयाय नमः

Any victory gained by the devotee, is a victory brought about by Him.

182. Vyavyasaya: *Strenuous Effort*

ॐ व्यवसायाय नमः

The prerequisite to victory is labour and staunch determination.

183. Atandrita: *The Ever Active*

ॐ अतन्द्रिताय नमः

He never sleeps — He is ever awake and active.

184. Adharshana: *The Unassailable*

ॐ अधर्षणाय नमः

He is invincible, being the embodiment of Eternal Time.

185. Dharshanatma: *The Aggressor*

ॐ धर्षणात्मने नमः

He spells terror to the violators of *Dharma*.

186. Yajnaha: *The Destroyer Of The Sacrificial Fire*

ॐ यज्ञघ्ने नमः

He is the Destroyer of the sacrificial fire of Daksha, father of Sati.

187. Kamanashaka: *The Destroyer Of Lust*

ॐ कामनाशकाय नमः

He is above all carnal pleasure, as He is Pure Consciousness, and hence destroys lust in one.

188. Dakshayagapahari: *The Destroyer Of Daksha's Sacrifice*

ॐ दक्षयागापहारये नमः

His destruction of Daksha's sacrificial fire suggests that a permissive or indulgent life leads to self-destruction.

189. Susaha: *Pleasant Endurance*

ॐ सुसहाय नमः

Lord Shiva, who is beyond comparison, and endowed with a pleasant endurance, is Eternal Bliss.

190. Madhyama: *The Impartial*

ॐ मध्यमाय नमः

He is attributeless, without likes and dislikes, and hence impartial.

191. Tejopahari: *The Withholder Of splendour*

ॐ तेजोपहारिने नमः

He showers His grace on only those who truly worship Him.

192. Balaha: *The Slayer Of Braggart's Strength*

ॐ बलघ्ने नमः

He punishes haughtiness and pride by robbing the beings of their strength.

29

193. Mudita: *The Delightful*

ॐ मुदिताय नमः

He with his auspicious and radiant graces, delights His devotees.

194. Artha: *The Wealth*

ॐ अर्थाय नमः

He is a storehouse of wealth, which He showers on the blessed.

195. Ajita: *The Invincible*

ॐ अजिताय नमः

He is beyond defeat as He is the Eternal One.

196. Avara: *Unsurpassed In Adoration*

ॐ अवराय नमः

He commands great respect and adoration from all, and is matchless in adoration and laudation.

197. Gambhiraghosha: *The Majestic Sound*

ॐ गम्भीरघोषाय नमः

Lord Shiva, the Creator of sound, is the fount of knowledge from whom the musical, majestic and divine sound carries revelations and the truth.

198. Gambhira: *The Profound*

ॐ गम्भीराय नमः

He is the Ocean of bliss that is profound and eternal.

199. Gambhirabalavahan: *Excellent Army And Vehicle*

ॐ गम्भीरबलवाहनाय नमः

He is the Supreme Commander of the army, and of Nandi, His bull-vehicles.

200. Nygrodharupa: *The Banyan*

ॐ न्यग्रोधरूपाय नमः

The banyan, representing the tree of *samsara*, has its root up in the Brahman, and branches down in the phenomenon.

201. Nyagrodha: *The Banyan*

ॐ न्यग्रोधाय नमः

Here, this is the banyan under which Dakshinamurti attained *Samadhi*.

202. Vrukshakarnasthiti: *Sleeper On A Banyan Leaf*

ॐ वृक्षकर्णस्थिताय नमः

Lord Shiva, ever awake and active, sleeps on a banyan leaf, suggesting that sleep is illusory, as He is the Master-Wielder of illusion.

203. Vibhu: *The Omnipresent*

ॐ विभवे नमः

He is all-pervasive, dwelling in every bit of space.

204. Sutheekshnadashana: *With Sharp Teeth*

ॐ सुतीक्ष्णदशनाय नमः

The tender and fair-skinned Lord Shiva has sharp teeth, capable of tearing the demons into shreds.

205. Mahakaya: *Huge-bodied*

ॐ महाकायाय नमः

He is majestic with His huge-bodied appearance.

206. Mahanan: *Huge-faced*

ॐ महाननाय नमः

The Divine Lord has a huge face that radiates happiness and reflects His purity.

207. Vishvaksena: *Whose Approach Scattered The Enemy Forces*

ॐ विष्वक्सेनाय नमः

Lord Shiva, the Supreme Commander, creates terror in the enemy forces when they see Him, and they flee in fear.

208. Hari: *The Remover Of Evil*

ॐ हरये नमः

He is the Scorcher of all wrongs, sins and evil.

209. Yajna: *Sacrifice*

ॐ यज्ञाय नमः

Lord Shiva, the Great Ascetic, dwells wherever there is self-denial.

210. Sanyugapidavahana: *Bull-ensign And Bull-vehicle*

ॐ संयुगापीडवाहनाय नमः

His divine vehicle is the bull, Nandi, and His pennant is the bull.

211. Teekshanatapa: *The Intensively Hot Fire*

ॐ तीक्ष्णतापाय नमः

He with His third eye on His forehead, scorches everything impure with an intense heat emanating from the eye.

212. Haryashva: *Possessing Green Horses*

ॐ हर्यश्वाय नमः

He shines brilliantly in the form of the Sun God having green horses.

213. Sahaya: *The Friend*

ॐ सहायाय नमः

He is the True Friend of beings in distress.

214. Karmakalavit: *The Knower Of The Right Time*

ॐ कर्मकालविदे नमः

Lord Shiva, the Controller of Time, knows the proper time for any action.

215. Vishnuprasadita: *Propitiated By Vishnu*

ॐ विष्णुप्रसादिताय नमः

He who obtained the famous chakra for Vishnu, is propitiated by the Lord.

216. Yajna: *Vishnu*

ॐ यज्ञाय नमः

Lord Shiva, who manifests in various forms, is also in the form of Vishnu.

217. Samudra: *The Ocean*

ॐ समुद्राय नमः

He is the Ocean of bliss, which signifies Infinitude.

218. Badavamukha: *The Heat In The Ocean*

ॐ बडवामुखाय नमः

There is a divine fire in Him which is like the warm heat in the ocean.

219. Hutashanasahaya: *The Wind, Fire's Friend*

ॐ हुताशनसहायाय नमः

Being the basic elements necessary for existence, He is the Controller of these elements which are in harmony with each other.

220. Prashantatma: *Calm-minded*

ॐ प्रशान्तात्मने नमः

As the Controller of the senses, He is ever calm and pleasant.

221. Hutashana: *The Fire*

ॐ हुताशनाय नमः

As Controller of the five elements, He manifests as Fire whenever the need arises.

222. Ugrateja: *The Fierce Splendour*

ॐ उग्रतेजसे नमः

He is the Terrible Fire that consumes the cosmos during *pralaya* or the great deluge, which leads to dissolution.

223. Mahateja: *The Great Splendour*

ॐ महातेजसे नमः

He dazzles in great splendour and brilliance, beyond comparison.

33

224. Janya: *The War-talented*

ॐ जन्याय नमः

Lord Shiva, the Supreme Commander of the forces, is extremely talented to win any war single-handedly.

225. Vijayakalavit: *The Knower Of The Time Of Victory*

ॐ विजयकालविदे नमः

Lord Shiva, the Controller of time, knows the right time and action for victory.

226. Tyotishamayanam: *Astrology*

ॐ ज्योतिषामयनाय नमः

He is the Source and Basis of the science of astrology.

227. Siddhi: *Accomplishment*

ॐ सिद्धये नमः

He is the Great Achiever and Accomplisher, and is propitiated before any action.

228. Sarvavigraha: *All Forms Are His*

ॐ सर्वविग्रहाय नमः

All the forms and shapes that are in existence are His.

229. Shikhi: *The Owner Of A Tuft*

ॐ शिखिने नमः

Lord Shiva, the Householder, bears a tuft in which is concealed the sacred Ganga.

230. Mundi: *The Shaven One*

ॐ मुण्डिने नमः

He with a clean-shaven head, is the Great Ascetic.

231. Jati: *With Matted Hair*

ॐ जटिने नमः

He with hair matted, is austere and simple like the forest-folk.

232. Jwali: *Fiery Rays*

ॐ ज्वालिने नमः

He blazes in all His glory, the fiery rays reflecting Pure Consciousness.

233. Murtija: *The Embodied*

ॐ मूर्तिजाय नमः

Lord Shiva, as we mortals know Him most, is in the human form.

234. Murdhaga: *Resident In The Head*

ॐ मूर्धगाय नमः

His residence is in the head.

235. Bali: *The Strong*

ॐ बलिने नमः

He is the Great Lord of divine power and immeasurable strength.

236. Vainavi: *The Holder Of Flute*

ॐ वैणविने नमः

Lord Shiva, who is fond of divine music, plays the flute, representing the primeval outburst of creation.

237. Panavi: *Possessing A Drum*

ॐ पणविने नमः

His small drum is the symbol of rhythm and sound.

238. Tali: *The Owner Of Cymbals*

ॐ तालिने नमः

He has in His possession various musical instruments that denote His love of music.

239. Khali: *The Owner Of Granaries*

ॐ खलिने नमः

Being the Lord of wealth, He sustains the three worlds, never keeping anyone in want.

240. Kalakatamkata: *One Who Conceals Yama*

ॐ कालकटंकटाय नमः

He alonen knows the mystery surrounding death.

241. Nakshatravigrahamati: *The Knower Of The Wheel Of Time*

ॐ नक्षत्रविग्रहमतये नमः

Lord Shiva, who controls time, knows the past, present and future.

242. Gunabuddhi: *The Virtuous Being*

ॐ गुणबुद्धये नमः

He is Pure Consciousness, the only Reality.

243. Laya: *The Abode Of Dissolution*

ॐ लयाय नमः

He being the Abode of dissolution, sees the apparent world by His all-pervading sight.

244. Agama: *The Stationary*

ॐ अगमाय नमः

He causing the rhythmic movement of the universe, is Himself stationary.

245. Prajapati: *The Lord Of Creature*

ॐ प्रजापतये नमः

He having cseated the three worlds, is the Lord of their inhabitants.

246. Vishwabahu: *The Multi-armed*

ॐ विश्वबाहवे नमः

He works through all the hands in the universe.

247. Vibhaga: *Apportionment*

ॐ विभागाय नमः

He combines in Himself the opposite qualities, i.e., the opposites in Him.

248. Sarvaga: *The Omnipresent*

ॐ सर्वगाय नमः

He makes His present felt in every nook and cranny of space.

249. Amukha: *The Mouthless*

ॐ अमुखाय नमः

The mouthless Lord Shiva is beyond bliss.

250. Vimochana: *The Deliver From Delusion*

ॐ विमोचनाय नमः

He is Absolute Reality and delivers beings from a world of delusion.

251. Susarana: *Easily Accessible*

ॐ सुसरणाय नमः

By meditating upon Him one can reach Him.

252. Hiranyakavachodbhava: *Manifest Through Golden Armour*

ॐ हिरण्यकवचोद्भवाय नमः

Lord Shiva, Wielder of the great *Maya*, manifests Himself through the veil of this *Maya*.

253. Meddraja: *Manifest From The Phallus*

ॐ मेढ्रजाय नमः

He manifests Himself in the form of a *linga* or phallus.

254. Balachari: *The Wood Dweller*

ॐ बलचारिने नमः

Arjuna met Lord Shiva who was in the guise of a Hunter.

255. Mahichari: *The Globe Trotter*

ॐ महीचारिने नमः

He ever wakeful, stalks the corners of the three worlds.

256. Sruta: *The Omnipresent*

ॐ सुताय नमः

He is all-pervading.

257. Sarvaturya Vinodi: *Delights In Orchestra*

ॐ सर्वतूर्य विनोदिने नमः

Having in His possession various musical instruments, He revels in orchestral music.

258. Sarvatodyaparigraha: *The Owner Of All Creatures*

ॐ सर्वतोद्यपरिग्रहाय नमः

He having created all creatures, is their Supreme Lord.

259. Vyalarupa: *The Serpent Adisesha*

ॐ व्यालरूपाय नमः

Lord Shiva, whose manifestations are many, also takes the form of the serpent, Adisesha, on whom reposes Vishnu.

260. Guhavasi: *The Cave-dweller*

ॐ गुहावासिने नमः

He dwells in the heart, which is the cave of every being.

261. Guha: *Subrahmanya*

ॐ गुहाय नमः

As the Preceptor of Lord Subrahmanya, or Kartikeya, He accepts the chants offered by His worshippers.

262. Mali: *Adorned With A Garland*

ॐ मालिने नमः

He is resplendent with snakes garlanding His glorious neck.

263. Tarangavit: *The Knower Of Waves*

ॐ तरंगविदे नमः

Just as waves appear and disappear, so do sense-enjoyments, and only He is aware of them.

264. Tridasha: *The Three States*

ॐ त्रिदशाय नमः

He is the three states of birth, sustenance and death.

265. Trikaladruk: *The Sustainer Of Time In Its Phases*

ॐ त्रिकालदृके नमः

He is the sustainer of the things of the past, present and future.

266. Karmasarva Bandhavimochana:

The Reliever Of The Bondage Of One's Karma

ॐ कर्मसर्वबन्धविमोचनाय नमः

He is magnanimous and compassionate, and relieves His devotees of their karmas.

267. Asurendranambandhana: *The Shackle Of Demonkings*

ॐ असुरेन्द्राणांबन्धनाय नमः

Lord Shiva, the Supreme Lord, is the Shackle that binds the demon-kings.

268. Yudhishatruvinashana: *The Destroyer Of Enemies In Battle*

ॐ युधिशत्रुविनाशनाय नमः

The Supreme Commander, Lord Shiva, vanquishes His enemies in the battlefield.

269. Sankhyaprasada: *The One Attained By Illumination*

ॐ सांख्यप्रसादाय नमः

He is the Self-lighted Omnipresent Being, who is attained only through the senses beyond perception.

270. Durvasa: *The Manifestation Of Durvasa*

ॐ दुर्वाससे नमः

He reveals Himself as Durvasa, the angry element in nature.

271. Sarvasadhunishevita: *Sought By Virtuous Men*

ॐ सर्वसाधुनिषेविताय नमः

He is revered and worshipped by all good people.

272. Praskandana: *The Exterminator*

ॐ प्रस्कन्दनाय नमः

During the pralaya (dissolution), He exterminates everything, Himself remaining Self-existent.

39

273. Vibhagajna: *The Intelligent Distributor*

ॐ विभागज्ञाय नमः

He is the intelligent and accurate Distributor of the fruits of one's actions.

274. Atulya: *The Incomparable*

ॐ अतुल्याय नमः

Lord Shiva, the supreme Divine Being, is beyond comparison.

275. Yajnabhagavit: *The Impartial Distributor*

ॐ यज्ञभागविदे नमः

He to whom everyone is equal, is the Impartial Distributor of the dues to the gods in the *yajna* or sacrificial offerings.

276. Sarvavasa: *The All-pervading*

ॐ सर्ववासाय नमः

He resides in every being, and everywhere.

277. Sarvachari: *The Wanderer Everywhere*

ॐ सर्वचारिने नमः

He ever awake and alert, is all-pervading, and loves to wander everywhere.

278. Durvasa: *The Naked*

ॐ दुर्वासे नमः

Lord Shiva, the Omnipresent, who cannot be clad, is clothed in space.

279. Vasava: *Indra*

ॐ वासवाय नमः

He with His dazzling brilliance, is Indra in one of His manifestations.

280. Amara: *The Immortal*

ॐ अमराय नमः

He is the Absolute Reality that ever was and, ever will be.

281. Haima: *The Snow*

ॐ हैमाय नमः

He is pure Consciousness, as pure as snow, and is realised only through the senses.

282. Hemakara: *The Maker Of Gold*

ॐ हेमकराय नमः

He dazzling like gold, is the Lord of wealth.

283. Nishkarma: *The Actionless*

ॐ निष्कर्माय नमः

He is the union of *ishwar* (substance — the life principle) and *shakti* (energy), and all *karmas* are attributed to *shakti*.

284. Sarvadhari: *The Upholder Of All*

ॐ सर्वधारिने नमः

Lord Shiva, the Supreme Being, sustains everybody and everything.

285. Dharothama: *The Best Bearer*

ॐ धरोत्तमाय नमः

Among all the bearers, like Adisesha, He is the best, for He bears the cosmos, Himself requiring no supports.

286. Lohitaksha: *The Red-eyed*

ॐ लोहिताक्षाय नमः

The red-eyed Shiva, from whose third eye emanates scorching fire, is all-seeing.

287. Mahaksha: *The Omni-perceiver*

ॐ महाक्षाय नमः

He ever wide awake and alert, sees everything, nothing being beyond His ken.

288. Vijayaksha: *The Victorious Chariot*

ॐ विजयाक्षाय नमः

He the Invincible, rides the victorious chariot.

41

289. Visharada: *The Learned*

ॐ विशारदाय नमः

Lord Shiva, the Originator of the *Vedas*, is the Source of all knowledge.

290. Sangraha: *The Guardian Of Devotees*

ॐ संग्रहाय नमः

Ever compassionate and bountiful, He is the Divine Guardian of His devotees.

291. Nigraha: *The Controller Of The Senses*

ॐ निग्रहाय नमः

As Lord of the organs, He controls the senses.

292. Karta: *The Actor*

ॐ कर्त्रे नमः

He is the Great Performer and the Source of all actions.

293. Sarpachiranivasana: *With Snakes For Belt*

ॐ सर्पचीरनिवासनाय नमः

He adorns snakes around His waist, and nothing in the universe is out of place in His cosmic Form.

294. Mukhya: *The Chief*

ॐ मुख्याय नमः

He is Supreme, the Lord of all.

295. Amukhya: *The Inferior*

ॐ अमुख्याय नमः

He who is the Source of the great and the small, is impartial, and in Him meet and combine all the opposites.

296. Deha: *The Body*

ॐ देहाय नमः

His body reveals auspiciousness.

297. Kahali: *The Owner Of A Large Drum*

ॐ काहलये नमः

The sound from the large drum of Lord Shiva comes from the word of Shiva, carrying revelations and the truth.

298. Sarvakamada: *The Granter Of All Desires*

ॐ सर्वकामदाय नमः

He is desirable and the Desire. He is the Lord who grants and fulfils all desires.

299. Sarvakalaprasada: *Always Kind*

ॐ सर्वकालप्रसादाय नमः

He the most compassionate and bountiful, is always kind to His devotees.

300. Subala: *The Beneficent Almighty*

ॐ सुबलाय नमः

The Beneficent and bountiful Shiva is the Supreme Lord.

301. Balarupadhrut: *Bearer Of Great Prowess And Beauty*

ॐ बलरूपधृते नमः

The handsome Shiva is known for His great prowess and beauty.

302. Sarvakamavara: *The Best Among The Desirables*

ॐ सर्वकामवराय नमः

Many are the desirables in the three worlds, but He stands out as the Best.

303. Sarvada: *The Bestower Of Everything*

ॐ सर्वदाय नमः

The ever-bountiful and compassionate Lord Shiva confers everything that His true devotees desire.

304. Sarvatomukha: *Having Faces Everywhere*

ॐ सर्वतोमुखाय नमः

He the All-pervading, faces in all directions, His vision being infinite.

305. Akashanirvirupa: *Like The Sky Manifests And Withdraws*

ॐ आकाशनिर्विरूपाय नमः

Just as Akash (sky) delineates, He manifests Beings out of Himself and withdraws them into Himself.

306. Nipati: *The Seemingly Fallen*

ॐ निपातिने नमः

He seems to have fallen into the filthy pit of the mortal being, but He is not actually so.

307. Avasha: *The Helpless*

ॐ अवशाय नमः

When the Self is identified with the body, It feels helpless, but in Itself, It is free.

308. Khaga: *The Bird*

ॐ खगाय नमः

The Self in the heart is free like the bird with no attachments.

309. Raudrarupa: *Of Terrible Form*

ॐ रद्रूरूपाय नमः

In the form of Rudra or Mahabhairava, only Lord Shiva is both beautiful and terrible.

310. Amshu: *The Sunbeam*

ॐ अंशवे नमः

Like the myriad beams of the sun, He dazzles in His glory.

311. Aditya: *The Sun*

ॐ आदित्याय नमः

He is the Sun, the Manifestation of light and energy that lights up every heart.

312. Bahurashmi: *The Myriad-rayed Sun*

ॐ बहुरश्मये नमः

Lord Shiva, Self-lighted, dazzles with the intensity of the myriad rays of the sun.

44

313. Suvarchasi: *Charming Effulgence*

ॐ सुवर्चसिने नमः

He is resplendent, radiating divine light and power.

314. Vasuvega: *The Speed Of The Wind*

ॐ वसुवेगाय नमः

He is everywhere, moving with the speed of the wind.

315. Mahavega: *The Great Speed*

ॐ महावेगाय नमः

He is the Great Speed without Whom nothing else moves.

316. Manovega: *The Speed Of The Mind*

ॐ मनोवेगाय नमः

Like the speed of the mind which is the fastest in the mundane, Lord Shiva, being all-pervading, is the fastest in all existence.

317. Nishachara: *The Night-wanderer*

ॐ निशाचराय नमः

The ever wakeful Lord Shiva wanders at night, when the rest of the world is asleep.

318. Sarvavasi: *Residing In All Bodies*

ॐ सर्ववासिने नमः

He resides in all bodies as the Self.

319. Shriyavasi: *The Dweller In Prosperity*

ॐ श्रियावासिने नमः

Lord Shiva, Lord of wealth, dwells in prosperity.

320. Upadeshakara: *The Bestower Of Knowledge*

ॐ उपदेशकराय नमः

Being the great Fount and Storehouse of knowledge, He bestows knowledge on His devotees.

321. Akara: *The Actionless*

ॐ अकराय नमः

All actions are part of nature, but Lord Shiva, the Doer, is Actionless.

322. Muni: *The Observer Of Silence*

ॐ मुनये नमः

Lord Shiva, the Greatest Ascetic, observes silence.

323. Atmaniraloka: *The Comprehensive Seer Of The Beings*

ॐ आत्मनिरालोकाय नमः

He knows well the past, present and future of the beings, for He is the Controller Of time.

324. Sambhagna: *The Well-adored*

ॐ संभग्नाय नमः

Lord Shiva, the Beneficent, is well adored and revered by everyone.

325. Sahasrada: *The Bestower In Plenty*

ॐ सहस्रदाय नमः

The ever Bountiful Lord Shiva bestows everything in plenty.

326. Pakshi: *The Bird Garuda*

ॐ पक्षिने नमः

He in one of His various manifestations, is Garuda, the divine vehicle of Vishnu.

327. Paksharupa: *The Benevolent Friend*

ॐ पक्षरूपाय नमः

He is the Benevolent Friend, most sought after by all.

328. Atideepta: *The Extremely Brilliant*

ॐ अतिदीप्ताय नमः

He is resplendent, like the concentrated rays of thousands of suns.

329. Vishampati: *The Lord Of Beings*

ॐ विशाम्पतये नमः

Lord Shiva, the Supreme Being, is the Lord of beings.

330. Unmada: *Love Intoxication*

ॐ उन्मादाय नमः

Lord Shiva, the Embodiment of love, showers love on all, the love which is intoxicating.

331. Madana: *The God Of Love*

ॐ मदनाय नमः

Cupid, the god of love, has his origin in Lord Shiva.

332. Kama: *Loved By All*

ॐ कामाय नमः

Lord Shiva, loved and worshipped by all, showers His grace on the hapless.

333. Aswaththa: *Peepal Tree*

ॐ अश्वत्थाय नमः

The peepal tree, with its spreading branches and roots, significant of a family, has its origin in Him.

334. Arthakara: *The Giver Of Wealth*

ॐ अर्थकराय नमः

Lord Shiva, the Lord of wealth, is most bountiful and liberal.

335. Yasha: *The Bestower Of Fame*

ॐ यशसे नमः

Lord Shiva, the most adored Supreme Being, bestows fame on the deserving.

336. Vamadeva: *The Allotter Of The Fruits Of Action*

ॐ वामदेवाय नमः

He apportions the fruits of one's action.

337. Vama: *The Noble*

ॐ वामाय नमः

Lord Shiva, the veritable Nemesis for evil-doers, is most noble and kind-hearted.

338. Prak: *The Eldest*

ॐ प्राचे नमः

Lord Shiva, the Supreme, has no one older than Him.

339. Dakshina: *The Skilful*

ॐ दक्षिणाय नमः

Lord Shiva, wielder of the great *maya*, is skilful and adroit.

47

340. Vamana: *The Dwarf*

ॐ वामनाय नमः

Lord Shiva and Vishnu being One, He came as Vamana to subdue Bali.

341. Siddhayogi: *The Mystic*

ॐ सिद्धयोगिने नमः

Lord Shiva, the Great Mystic who wields *maya*, is Absolute Reality.

342. Maharshi: *The Highly Enlightened One*

ॐ महर्षये नमः

Lord Shiva is the Supremely Wise, the highly Enlightened One.

343. Siddhartha: *The Accomplisher Of Everything*

ॐ सिद्धार्थाय नमः

Lord Shiva, personifying success, accomplishes everything successfully.

344. Siddhasadhaka: *The Bestower Of Siddhas*

ॐ सिद्धसाधकाय नमः

He bestows success on the devotees who adore and worship Him.

345. Bhikshu: *The Mendicant*

ॐ भिक्षवे नमः

He is the Greatest Ascetic, and personifies perfection.

346. Bhikshurupa: *Holy Mendicant*

ॐ भिक्षुरूपाय नमः

He manifests Himself as the Perfect Holy Mendicant.

347. Vipana: *Without The Marks Of An Ascetic*

ॐ विपणाय नमः

Lord Shiva, though the perfect Ascetic, is yet without the signs of one.

348. Mrudu: *The Soft-hearted*

ॐ मृदवे नमः

He is extremely noble and soft-hearted, being very compassionate and bounteous.

48

349. Avyaya: *The Changeless*

ॐ अव्ययाय नमः

He is the source of all changes and Himself remains changeless.

350. Mahasena: *The Celestial Commander*

ॐ महासेनाय नमः

He is the Supreme Celestial Commander who stands for victory.

351. Vishakha: *Youthful*

ॐ विशारखाय नमः

As the Youthful Lord, He once helped Indra when he was in trouble.

352. Shastthibhaga: *Sixty Parts*

ॐ षष्ठिभागाय नमः

The functions of the senses are said to be sixty, and He is the Lord of all.

353. Gavampati: *The Propeller Of Senses*

ॐ गवांपतये नमः

Lord Shiva, being the Lord of the senses, controls them, prodding them on for awareness.

354. Vajrahasta: *The Propeller Of Senses*

ॐ वज्रहस्ताय नमः

Lord Shiva, wielding the *vajra*, the thunder-bolt, controls all by destroying their egos and pride.

355. Vishkambhi: *The Support*

ॐ विष्कम्भिने नमः

He is the rock-like Support who sustains all.

356. Chamustambhana: *The Stupifier Of The Enemies*

ॐ चमूस्तम्भनाय नमः

He is the Invincible, who with His *maya* stupefies the enemies.

357. Vrathhavrathhakara: *The Chariot Warfare Expert*

ॐ वृत्तावृत्तकराय नमः

He is adept in handling the chariot during warfare.

358. Tala: *The Basis Of The Phenomenon*

ॐ तालाय नमः

Lord Shiva, the Source of everything, is the Basis of the mundane and the spiritual.

359. Madhu: *The Spring Season*

ॐ मधवे नमः

He is the Great Controller of time, and as the Spring Season heralds all that is auspicious and lovely.

360. Madhukalochana: *The Red-eyed*

ॐ मधुकलोचनाय नमः

Lord Shiva, the all-seeing, is the red-eyed Supreme Lord, embodying higher perception.

361. Vachaspati: *The Family Priest*

ॐ वाचस्पतये नमः

Lord Shiva, personifying auspiciousness, is propitiated before the commencement of an event, for, like the family priest, His wisdom is sought.

362. Vajasana: *The Preceptor Of Vajaseniya*

ॐ वाजसनाय नमः

He is the Source of the Vajaseniya which is a branch of the sacred *Vedas*.

363. Nityamashrita Pujita: *Ever Worshipped By Devotees*

ॐ नित्यमाश्रित पूजिताय नमः

He is the favourite Deity and is always worshipped and revered by them.

364. Brahmachari: *Devoted To Brahman*

ॐ ब्रह्मचारिणे नमः

He in His various manifestations, is deeply devoted to Brahman.

365. Lokachari: *The Itinerant Mendicant*

ॐ लोकचारिणे नमः

Lord Shiva, the Supreme Ascetic following austere measures, wanders over the earth, keeping vigil over the lesser beings.

366. Sarvachari: *The All-pervading Reality*

ॐ सर्वचारिणे नमः

Lord Shiva, who moves everywhere while remaining everywhere, is the Self of everything.

367. Vicharavit: *The Introvert*

ॐ विचारविदे नमः

He is the Supreme Self who knows the ways of introspection.

368. Ishana: *The Inner Ruler*

ॐ ईशानाय नमः

He is the Inner Ruler, dwelling in every being as the Self.

369. Ishwara: *The Lord*

ॐ इश्वराय नमः

The Supreme Lord Shiva is Absolute Reality.

370. Kala: *Time*

ॐ कालाय नमः

Lord Shiva, like Chandragupta, metes out justice according to one's acts of good and bad.

371. Nishachari: *Ever Awake*

ॐ निशाचारिणे नमः

In dissolution, when the whole cosmos is at rest at night, He is ever wakeful and alert.

372. Pinakavan: *Armed With Pinaka*

ॐ पिनाकाभृते नमः

Lord Shiva, armed with the divine bow, Pinaka, is the Saviour of His devotees.

373. Nimithastha: *Resider In The Target*

ॐ निमित्तस्थाय नमः

He is the Shooter, the Bow and the Target (the Daityas).

374. Nimitam: *The Cause*

ॐ निमिताय नमः

He is the Source from Whom all else is caused.

375. Nanda: *The Happy One*

ॐ नन्दाय नमः

Lord Shiva, the Repository of wealth, is ever blissful.

376. Nandakara: *The Creator Of Happiness*

ॐ नन्दकराय नमः

Lord Shiva, the Creator of happiness, confers wealth in plenty.

377. Hari: *The Monkey God, Anjaneya*

ॐ हरये नमः

Anjaneya, the help of Lord Rama, has the form of a monkey, but with a perfect mental balance. Likewise is Lord Shiva.

378. Nandishwara: *The Lord Of Nandi*

ॐ नन्दीश्वराय नमः

He is the Lord of His vehicle, Nandi.

379. Nandi: *The Vehicle Nandi*

ॐ नन्दिने नमः

Lord Shiva, who dwells in all, is Nandi, the vehicle.

380. Nandana: *The Promoter of Happiness*

ॐ नन्दनाय नमः

Lord Shiva, personifying eternal bliss, brings joy to all.

381. Nandivardhana: *Enhancer Of Joy*

ॐ नन्दिवर्धनाय नमः

He enhances the bliss of the devotees.

382. Bhagahari: *The Destroyer Of Wealth*

ॐ भगहारिणे नमः

He takes away the wealth and status of even Indra and other gods.

383. Nihanta: *The Destroyer Of Life*

ॐ निहन्त्रे नमः

Lord Shiva, the Procreator and Sustainer of all life, is also the Destroyer.

384. Kala: *The Storehouse Of Arts*

ॐ कालाय नमः

Arts, which are believed to be sixty-four in number, have their origin in Him.

385. Brahma: *The Great*

ॐ ब्रह्मणे नमः

None else is greater than Lord Shiva.

386. Pitamaha: *The Grand Sire*

ॐ पितामहाय नमः

He is the Grand Sire, the Universal Master whose word is law.

387. Chaturmukha: *The Four-faced*

ॐ चतुर्मुखाय नमः

He is the four-faced Brahma, as He is all-in-all.

388. Mahalinga: *The Great Symbol*

ॐ महालिंगाय नमः

He is the Great Symbol worshipped universally with great devotion.

389. Charulinga: *The Beautiful Symbol*

ॐ चारूलिंगाय नमः

Lord Shiva, embodying the beautiful symbol, is of attractive countenance.

390. Lingadhyaksha: *The Master Of the Symbols*

ॐ लिंगाध्यक्षाय नमः

He is the apt presiding symbol, both for manifestation through procreation and dissolution through renunciation.

391. Suradhyaksha: *Presiding Over The Gods*

ॐ सुराध्यक्षाय नमः

Lord Shiva, the Lord of the gods, presides over the senses.

392. Yogadhyaksha: *The Lord Of Yoga*

ॐ योगाध्यक्षाय नमः

He is the Ruler of unification (yoga) which becomes possible only through His grace.

393. Yugavaha: *The Creator Of Yugas*

ॐ युगावहाय नमः

He is the Creator of the Yugas — Krita, Treta, Dvapara and Kali — which extend over long periods.

394. Bijadhyaksha: *The Lord Of Seeds*

ॐ बीजाध्यक्षाय नमः

Lord Shiva, controlling nature, regulates virtue and vice, and dispenses their effects.

395. Bijakarta: *The Creator Of Nature*

ॐ बीजकर्त्रे नमः

Lord Shiva, the Creator of virtue and vice, causes nature to manifest itself.

396. Adhyatamanugata: *The Follower Of Self-knowledge*

ॐ अध्यात्मानुगताय नमः

Lord Shiva, being the Aspirant of the science of the soul, is the follower of self-knowledge.

397. Bala: *Fortitude*

ॐ बलाय नमः

Lord Shiva, the Greatest Mendicant, is endowed with great fortitude.

398. Itihasa: *The Epics*

ॐ इतिहासाय नमः

He embodies the Great Epics — the *Ramayana* and the *Mahabharata*.

399. Sakalpa: *Rituals in Mimamsa*

ॐ सकल्पाय नमः

Rituals, associated with the rules of sacrifice, as prescribed in the Mimamsa system, are to be followed strictly to be able to attain to the Great Lord.

400. Gautama: *The Founder Of Logic*

ॐ गोतमाय नमः

He is the Promulgator of logic, and controls the five senses.

401. Nishakara: *The Moon*

ॐ निशाकराय नमः

Lord Shiva, in the form of a Rishi, founded the school of grammarians called Chandra Vyakarana

402. Dambha: *The Subduer*

ॐ दम्भाय नमः

He is deathless and ever victorious — no enemy can escape from His subjugation.

403. Adambha: *Whom None Can Control*

ॐ अदम्भाय नमः

Lord Shiva, the Divine Almighty, is beyond the control of anyone.

404. Vaidambha: *The Self Of The Humble*

ॐ वैदम्भाय नमः

He is the Soul of those devoid of any pride, and to be free from hypocrisy is a divine gift.

405. Vashya: *Amenable To The Devotees*

ॐ वश्याय नमः

Lord Shiva, always docile and gentle, is amenable to His devotees.

406. Vashakara: *The Influencer*

ॐ वशकराय नमः

Lord Shiva, the Great Captivator, influences everyone by His austerity and uprighteousness.

407. Kali: *The Formenter Of Quarrels*

ॐ कलये नमः

He forments the strife between gods and demons—between the good and the evil.

408. Lokakarta: *The Creator Of The Worlds*

ॐ लोककर्त्रे नमः

As Creator of the three worlds, He is the Supreme Brahman, without decay and change.

409. Pashupati: *The Lord Of Beings*

ॐ पशुपतये नमः

Lord Shiva, being compassionate and kind, protects all beings.

410. Mahakarta: *The Creator Of The Five Elements*

ॐ महाकर्त्रे नमः

Lord Shiva, with whom the world is instinct, is the Creator of the five elements—water, air, earth, fire and ether.

411. Anaushadha: *The One Who Eats Not*

ॐ अनौषधाय नमः

Since He is Supra-mundane, He neither grows nor decays, and hence he does not eat.

412. Aksharam: *The Imperishable*

ॐ अक्षराय नमः

Lord Shiva, beyond decay, is imperishable.

413. Paramam Brahma: *The Supreme Brahman*

ॐ परमाय ब्रह्मणे नमः

Lord Shiva, the Supreme Brahman, is Pure Bliss.

414. Balavan: *The Strong*

ॐ बलवते नमः

He is the Supreme Deity presiding over strength.

415. Shakra: *Indra*

ॐ शक्राय नमः

He is also Indra, the Lord of Devas.

416. Neeti: *Punishment*

ॐ नित्यै नमः

He is the Punishment on those that deserve to be punished.

417. Aneeti: *Injustice*

ॐ अनित्यै नमः

The tyranny prevailing in the world is His power that is mishandled.

418. Shuddhatma: *The Pure-minded*

ॐ शुद्धात्मने नमः

Lord Shiva, the most auspicious, is pure-minded and, hence, Absolute Bliss.

419. Shuddha: *The Pure*

ॐ शुद्धाय नमः

He can be tainted by none — He is absolutely pure.

420. Manya: *The Worshipful*

ॐ मान्याय नमः

Lord Shiva, most worshipful, is adored by His devotees.

421. Gatagata: *The Cycle*

ॐ गतागताय नमः

He is that Eternal Cycle, the World that goes and comes eternally.

422. Bahuprasada: *Immensely Auspicious*

ॐ बहुप्रसादाय नमः

Lord Shiva, with limitless attributes, is immensely auspicious, and invoked by all for success.

423. Suswapna: *Good Dream*

ॐ सुस्वप्नाय नमः

Good dreams are signs of mind-purification, over which He presides.

424. Darpana: *The Mirror*

ॐ दर्पणाय नमः

He is Pure Consciousness, and like a mirror, reflects the universe.

425. Amritajit: *Conqueror Of The Enemies*

ॐ अमित्रजिते नमः

He is the Conqueror of the enemies, both internal and external, the internal being the bad tendencies that lead one to evil ways.

426. Vedakara: *The Maker Of The Vedas*

ॐ वेदकाराय नमः

The Author Of the *Vedas*, Lord Shiva, has the various branches of the *Vedas* as His breath.

427. Mantrakara: *The Maker Of The Mantras*

ॐ श्री मन्त्रकाराय नमः

Lord Shiva is the Maker of the Mantras which are other than those found in the *Vedas* — the Tantras, the Puranas, etc.

428. Vidwan: *The Learned*

ॐ विदुषे नमः

Lord Shiva, the Greatest Scholar, dwells in all as Divinity, manifesting well in the learned.

429. Samaramardana: *The Vanquisher Of Foes In Wars*

ॐ समरमर्दनाय नमः

Lord Shiva, the Unconquerable and the Deathless, vanquishes His foes in wars.

430. Mahameghanivasi: *The Dweller In the Great Clouds*

ॐ महामेघनिवासिने नमः

When the worlds dissolve during the great deluge, He dwells in the great clouds as their Presiding Deity.

58

431. Mahaghora: *The Most Terrible*

ॐ महाघोराय नमः

He is terrible at the time of deluge.

432. Vashi: *The Subjugator Of All*

ॐ वशिने नमः

As the Lord of all beings He subjugates them.

433. Kara: *The Destroyer*

ॐ कराय नमः

Lord Shiva, the Lord of Destructions, delights in destruction for its own sake.

434. Agnijwala: *Flaming As Fire*

ॐ अग्निज्वालाय नमः

Lord Shiva, at the time of dissolution, manifests as the Great Flames of Fire.

435. Mahajwala: *The Great Flames*

ॐ महाज्वालाय नमः

As Lord of Destruction, He is the Great Flames that rage during dissolution.

436. Atidhumra: *All Smoke*

ॐ अतिधूम्राय नमः

Lord Shiva, as the Great Fire of Time, burns up everything, with smoke emanating fiercely.

437. Huta: *Pleased With Offerings*

ॐ हुताय नमः

He is pleased with every act of self-sacrifice or self-denial.

438. Havi: *The Offering*

ॐ हविशे नमः

He is the Offering in sacrifice, and ownership is sacrificed by offering back His things to Him with affection and ardour.

439. Vrushana: *The Fountain Of Virtue*

ॐ वृषणाय नमः

The uprighteous draw inspiration from Him Who is the Fountain of virtue.

440. Shankara: *The Doer Of Good*

ॐ शंकराय नमः

He as the Beneficent Deity, is the Doer of all good things.

441. Nityamvarchasvi: *Ever Radiant*

ॐ नित्यंवर्चस्विने नमः

He is the ever radiant and energetic Supreme Being.

442. Dhoomaketana: *Smoky Fire*

ॐ धूमकेतनाय नमः

He is the Great Fire clouded with smoke.

443. Neela: *Blue*

ॐ नीलाय नमः

Like a blue gem, He sparkles with radiant lustre.

444. Angalubdha: *Ever Present In His Linga*

ॐ अंगलुब्धाय नमः

He remains in His limbs, and is ever present in His Form.

445. Shobhana: *Auspicious*

ॐ शोभनाय नमः

He is the Essence of everything pure and auspicious.

446. Niravagraha: *The Granter Of All Desires*

ॐ निरवग्रहाय नमः

He is the spontaneous Giver of all the desired objects.

447. Swastida: *The Bestower Of Prosperity*

ॐ स्वस्तिदाय नमः

Lord Shiva, the ever Bountiful, confers prosperity on the deserving.

448. Swastibhava: *The Supreme Being*

ॐ स्वस्तिभावाय नमः

He is the Absolute Supreme Being, beyond comparison.

449. Bhagi: *The Sharer In Sacrifices*

ॐ भागिने नमः

Lord Shiva, the Great Ascetic, partakes in the sacrifices.

450. Bhagakara: *Distributor Of The Shares*

ॐ भागकराय नमः

During sacrifices, He distributes the shares of the sacrificial offerings among the gods.

451. Laghu: *Quick*

ॐ लघवे नमः

He is quick in extending grace.

452. Utsanga: *The Unattached*

ॐ उत्संगाय नमः

He is detached from all mundane matters, remaining unaffected by anything.

453. Mahanga: *The Mighty-limbed*

ॐ महांगाय नमः

Lord Shiva of the great symbols is the mighty-limbed Conqueror of evil.

454. Mahagarbhaparayana: *The God Of Love*

ॐ महागर्भपरायणाय नमः

He is the Great Womb of the universe during the deluge, and the Supreme Goal.

455. Krishnavarna: *The Dark Complexioned*

ॐ कृष्णवर्णाय नमः

He manifests as the dark-complexioned as Vishnu, for Shiva-Vishnu-Brahma is but One God.

456. Suvarna: *The White-complexioned*

ॐ सुवर्णाय नमः

Lord Shiva, in His manifestation as Shambhu, is fair-complexioned.

457. Sarvadehinamindriya: *The Senses Of All Embodied Beings*

ॐ सर्वदेहिनाम् इन्द्रियाय नमः

As Lord of the senses, He resides in all as their senses.

458. Mahapada: *Of Great Feet*

ॐ महापादाय नमः

Lord Shiva, the mighty-limbed, is the Owner of great feet.

459. Mahahasta: *Of Great Hands*

ॐ महाहस्ताय नमः

He is endowed with great hands that bless the deserving.

460. Mahakaya: *Of A Great Body*

ॐ महाकायाय नमः

He is constituted with the Cosmic Body.

461. Mahayasha: *Of Universal Fame*

ॐ महायशसे नमः

Lord Shiva, as the most favoured among the deities, has great universal fame.

462. Mahamurdha: *Of A Great Head*

ॐ महामूर्ध्ने नमः

He is endowed with the great universal head.

463. Mahamatra: *Of Great Dimensions*

ॐ महामात्राय नमः

Lord Shiva, the Attributeless, is of great dimensions, beyond measure.

464. Mahanetra: *Of A Penetrating Vision*

ॐ महानेत्राय नमः

He sees all, penetrating into the core of everything.

465. Nishalaya: *The Destroyer Of Ignorance*

ॐ निशालयाय नमः

He destroys ignorance and offers refuge to His devotees, thus dispelling darkness.

466. Mahantaka: *The Great Death*

ॐ महान्तकाय नमः

He is the Dealer of death, to even Yama.

467. Mahakarna: *Of Great Ears*

ॐ महाकर्णाय नमः

He is endowed with great ears that hear everything.

468. Mahoshttha: *Of Great Lips*

ॐ महोष्ठाय नमः

Lord Shiva, endowed with great lips, is ever-smiling.

469. Mahahanu: *Of Mighty Cheeks And Jaws*

ॐ महाहनवे नमः

Lord Shiva, the handsome, mighty Conqueror, is captivating with His beautiful, large cheeks and jaws.

470. Mahanasa: *Of A Great Nose*

ॐ महानासाय नमः

Lord Shiva, with a prominent nose, enthrals all with His mighty presence.

471. Mahakambu: *Of A Great Throat*

ॐ महाकम्बवे नमः

He is endowed with the all-consuming throat.

472. Mahagriva: *Of A Great Neck*

ॐ महाग्रीवाय नमः

Lord Shiva, the Possessor of a great blue neck, is fair and handsome.

473. Shmashanabhak: *Lord Of The Cremation Ground*

ॐ श्मशानभाजे नमः

Lord Shiva, the Great Ascetic, is the remover of the bondage of the bodies.

474. Mahavaksha: *Of A Great Chest*

ॐ महावक्षसे नमः

He blesses those devotees whose chests are dedicated to the protection of the good.

475. Mahoraska: *The Great Bosom*

ॐ महोरस्काय नमः

He gives refuge in His great bosom to His true ones who harbour divine ideas.

476. Antaratma: *The Inner Soul*

ॐ अन्तरात्मने नमः

He dwells in every being as the Inner Soul.

477. Mrugalaya: *Adorned With The Deer*

ॐ मृगलयाय नमः

Lord Shiva, holding aloft a deer, blesses them that cognise the presence of the Divinity within.

478. Lambana: *From Whom Hangs The Universe*

ॐ लम्बनाय नमः

The universe hangs from Him like fruits from a tree.

479. Lambitoshttha: *With Projected Lips*

ॐ लम्बितोष्ठाय नमः

Lord Shiva, at the time of dissolution, protrudes His lips as if to swallow with gusto the universe.

480. Mahamaya: *The Mighty Illusion*

ॐ महामायाय नमः

He is the Possessor of the Delusion that keeps Brahma and others in bondage.

481. Payonidhi: *The Ocean Of Milk*

ॐ पयोनिधये नमः

He is the Ocean of milk, the Sustainer of beings in the universe.

482. Mahadanta: *Of Great Teeth*

ॐ महादन्ताय नमः

Lord Shiva, sporting great teeth, has the universal power of biting and masticating.

483. Mahadanshtra: *Of Great Fangs*

ॐ महादंष्ट्राय नमः

Lord Shiva, with great fangs, is symbolic of destruction.

484. Mahajihva: *Of A Great Tongue*

ॐ महाजिह्वाय नमः

Lord Shiva, with His great tongue held out, is symbolic of not being satiated with the swallowing of the universe.

485. Mahamukha: *Of A Great Face*

ॐ महामुखाय नमः

Lord Shiva, with a significant face that is expressive, embodies power, dignity and calmness.

486. Mahanakha: *Of Great Nails*

ॐ महानखाय नमः

He possesses highly powerful nails that indicate His destructive power.

487. Maharoma: *Of Great Hair*

ॐ महारोमाय नमः

Lord Shiva, in His Varaha, the boar, incarnation (as Vishnu) demonstrated the destructive power of the hair.

488. Mahakosha: *Of A Great Belly*

ॐ महाकोशाय नमः

The manifest and unmanifest are all contained in His great belly.

489. Mahajata: *Of Great Matted Locks*

ॐ महाजटाय नमः

His matted locks are indicative of the unconcern for bodily polish.

65

490. Prasanna: *Ever Cheerful*

ॐ प्रसन्नाय नमः

Lord Shiva, with a pleasant aspect, radiates cheer and joy around with His radiance.

491. Prasada: *Tranquillity And Favour*

ॐ प्रसादाय नमः

Personifying tranquillity, He presents a favourable demeanour.

492. Pratyaya: *Firm Conviction*

ॐ प्रत्ययाय नमः

He is the Experience and Firm Conviction that guide a being to realise the self.

493. Girisadhana: *With The Mountain As His Bow*

ॐ गिरिसाधनाय नमः

Lord Shiva, the Dweller of the mountains, uses the mountain as His bow.

494. Snehana: *Full Of Affection*

ॐ स्नेहनाय नमः

Like a father's affection for his children, His affection for His devotees is beyond question.

495. Asnehana: *Devoid Of Affection*

ॐ अस्नेहनाय नमः

Lord Shiva, the Unattached, can be completely detached, signifying that one can rise above mundane matters through detachment.

496. Ajita: *The Invincible*

ॐ अजिताय नमः

Lord Shiva, who has no equal or comparison, is invincible.

497. Mahamuni: *Extremely Silent*

ॐ महामुनये नमः

Being the Perfect Ascetic, He can be both silent and contemplative.

498. Vrukshakara: *Embodiment Of The Family Tree*

ॐ वृक्षाकाराय नमः

Lord Shiva, shaped like a tree, embodies the tree of *samsara*.

499. Vrukshaketu: *With The Symbol Of A Tree*

ॐ वृक्षकेतवे नमः

He is the Possessor of the tree-ensign. Representing *Samsara*, He can be known only through the body and organs.

500. Anala: *Fire*

ॐ अनलाय नमः

He is the fire that never has enough to consume.

501. Vayuvahana: *With The Air As His Vehicle*

ॐ वायुवाहनाय नमः

Lord Shiva, using the air as His vehicle to go from place to place, makes the wind blow.

502. Gandali: *Residing On Hills*

ॐ गण्डलिने नमः

Lord Shiva, the Lover of mountains, resides on elevated places.

503. Merudhama: *Resident Of Meru*

ॐ मेरूधाम्ने नमः

Lord Shiva, the Great Ascetic, resides on the Meru Mountain.

504. Devadhipati: *The Lord Of The Gods*

ॐ देवाधिपतये नमः

Lord Shiva, who is phaseless, perfect, unborn, is the Lord of the gods.

505. Atharvashirsha: *His Head As The Atharvans*

ॐ अथर्वशीर्षाय नमः

His head is the *Atharvopanishads*.

506. Samasya: *The Samaveda As Shiva's Face*

ॐ सामास्याय नमः

The Lord's face is the *Samaveda*.

507. Riksahasramitekshana: *Countless Risks Are His Large Eyes*

ॐ ऋक्सहस्त्रामितेक्षणाय नमः

Countless Rik Mantras are His boundless eyes.

508. Yajuhapadabhuja: *The Yajus Are His Limbs*

ॐ यजुःपादभुजाय नमः

His arms and feet are the Yajus.

509. Guhya: *The Upanishads Are His Secret Part*

ॐ गुह्याय नमः

He has the *Upanishads* as His subtle truth.

510. Prakasha: *The Rituals As Common Parts*

ॐ प्रकाशाय नमः

He is the Exotericism of the ritualistic section.

511. Jangama: *The Moveable*

ॐ जंगमाय नमः

All the mobile creatures are Lord Shiva — He is present in everyone.

512. Amoghartha: *Of Fruitful Request*

ॐ अमोघार्थाय नमः

Prayers to Him are ever fruitful. This aspect of Him is the Immanent Reality cognizable by the senses and intellect.

513. Prasada: *The Compassionate*

ॐ प्रसादाय नमः

The Great, Compassionate Lord Shiva is an unseen influence.

514. Abhigamya: *The Easily Attainable*

ॐ अभिगम्याय नमः

Lord Shiva, the most bountiful and compassionate, is easily attainable.

515. Sudarshana: *Of Auspicious Looks*

ॐ सुवर्शनाय नमः

Lord Shiva, with His fair complexion and attractive eyes, is beautiful to look at.

516. Upakara: *The Helpful*

ॐ उपकाराय नमः

He is ever helpful and considerate during trying times.

517. Priya: *The Beloved*

ॐ प्रियाय नमः

Lord Shiva, the Beloved, confers happiness on all.

518. Sarva: *The All*

ॐ सर्वाय नमः

Lord Shiva, the All-in-all, hastens towards the devotees who seek and approach Him.

519. Kanaka: *Gold*

ॐ कनकाय नमः

Lord Shiva, sparkling like gold, is valued dearer than gold by all.

520. Kanchancchavi: *The Golden-hued*

ॐ कांचनच्छवये नमः

Lord Shiva, brighter than the brightest object seen by man, is golden-hued.

521. Nabhi: *The Centre Of The Universe*

ॐ नाभये नमः

He is the Navel, the core of the universe.

522. Nandikara: *Cause of Plenty*

ॐ नन्दिकराय नमः

He is the Augmentor of the fruits of sacrifice.

523. Bhava: *Devotion To Sacrifice*

ॐ भावाय नमः

Lord Shiva, being the Greatest Ascetic, is devoted to sacrifice.

524. Pushkarasthapati: *The Architect Of The Lotus-shaped Universe*

ॐ पुष्करस्थपतये नमः

Lord Shiva, as beautiful as a lotus, is the Architect of the lotus-shaped universe.

69

525. Sthira: *Firm*

ॐ स्थिराय नमः

He is firm and constant.

526. Dwadasha: *The Twelfth Stage In Human Life*

ॐ व्दादशाय नमः

He is Salvation (*Moksha*) which is the twelfth stage in life, the first being taking life in the womb, the tenth being death, and the eleventh being attainment of heaven or *Swarga*.

527. Trasana: *The Creator Of Fear*

ॐ त्रासनाय नमः

Lord Shiva, who creates fear in the sinners, represents the intermediary states.

528. Adhya: *The First*

ॐ आद्याय नमः

He is the Origin, the Middle and the End, and nobody existed before Him.

529. Yajna: *The Union*

ॐ यज्ञाय नमः

He is the Union between the *Jiva* and Ishwara.

530. Yajnasamahita: *Attainable Through Yoga*

ॐ यज्ञसमाहिताय नमः

Lord Shiva, dwelling in the sacrifice, is attainable through yoga.

531. Naktam: *The Night*

ॐ नक्ताय नमः

He is the Great Illusion, the Night, causing the darkness of ignorance.

532. Kali: *The Strife*

ॐ कलये नमः

He is the Strife, manifesting desire and hatred.

70

533. Kala: *The Time*

ॐ कालाय नमः

He is the Time, causing the cycle of birth and death.

534. Makara: *The Symbol Of Time*

ॐ मकराय नमः

Lord Shiva, shaped like the *makara* or whale, is the Symbol of time.

535. Kalapujita: *Adored By Death*

ॐ कालपूजिताय नमः

Lord Shiva, representing the cycle of birth and death, is adored by Yama, the god of death.

536. Sagana: *Surrounded by Devotees*

ॐ सगणाय नमः

Lord Shiva, the most adored God, lives with His devotees.

537. Ganakara: *Including Others In His Unit*

ॐ गणकाराय नमः

He attracts more and more devotees to Himself.

538. Bhutavahanasarathi: *With Brahma As Charioteer*

ॐ भूतवाहनसारथये नमः

He has the Creator Brahma as His charioteer.

539. Bhasmashaya: *Reclining On The Holy Ashes*

ॐ भस्मशयाय नमः

The Holy ash is the best symbol of Shiva, as it cannot be further burnt, indicating the imperishability of the Reality.

540. Bhasmagopta: *Protector Through The Holy Ash*

ॐ भस्मगोप्त्रे नमः

He is the Holy Ash, signifying that when desires are burnt out, the Reality alone remains unaffected.

71

541. Bhasmabhuta: *Formed Of Ashes*

ॐ भस्मभूताय नमः

When Sage Munkanaka started dancing on seeing the vegetable juice drip from his hand, Lord Shiva, in order to stop his dance, showed him the holy ashes flowing from His body to prove that His body was composed of sacred ashes.

542. Taru: *The Tree*

ॐ तरवे नमः

He is the Divine Tree, offering shelter to the seekers.

543. Gana: *Attendants*

ॐ गणाय नमः

He is the Self in the attendants such as Bhringi, Riti, Nandi, etc.

544. Lokapala: *The Guardian Of The worlds*

ॐ लोकपालाय नमः

He is the Great Guardian of the worlds which number fourteen.

545. Aloka: *Transcending The Worlds*

ॐ अलोकाय नमः

Lord Shiva, the Lord and Guardian of the worlds, transcends these worlds.

546. Mahatma: *The Perfect Atman*

ॐ महात्मने नमः

He is the Perfect Soul, pure and imperishable.

547. Sarvapujita: *Worshipped By All*

ॐ सर्वपूजिताय नमः

Lord Shiva, worshipped by all, is the Pinnacle of devotion.

548. Shukla: *The Pure*

ॐ शुक्लाय नमः

He is the pure, absolute Reality.

549. Trishukla: *Threefold White*

ॐ त्रिशुक्लाय नमः

He is the Pure Reality, who expects His devotees to be pure in body, speech and mind.

550. Sampanna: *Complete Emancipation*

ॐ सम्पन्नाय नमः

He is complete Emancipation, or in other words, Total Salvation.

551. Shuchi: *Shining With Purity*

ॐ शुचये नमः

Lord Shiva, shining with purity, is undefiled by external impurities, signifying that He is unattached.

552. Bhutanishevita: *Worshipped By The Ancient Teachers*

ॐ भूतनिषेविताय नमः

Lord Shiva, the Adorable Lord, is worshipped by the ancient teachers.

553. Ashramastha: *Dweller In the Holy Orders*

ॐ आश्रमस्थाय नमः

He dwells as Dharma in the Holy Orders that are four in number.

554. Kriyavastha: *Resider In Rituals*

ॐ क्रियावस्थाय नमः

He dwells in rituals such as sacrifices that form the preparatory stage to the practice of *Dharma*.

555. Vishwakarmamati: *The Intelligence Of Vishwakarman*

ॐ विश्वकर्ममतये नमः

He is the Intelligence, the Skill of the architect in designing the universe.

556. Vara: *The Boon*

ॐ वराय नमः

He is the Boon most sought after.

557. Vishalashakha: *The Long-armed*

ॐ विशालशाखाय नमः

He is the long-armed Protector from death.

558. Tamroshttha: *The Red-lipped*

ॐ ताम्रोष्ठाय नमः

Lord Shiva, the red-lipped Deity, is extremely handsome.

559. Ambujala: *The Ocean*

ॐ अम्बुजालाय नमः

He is the Ocean significant of the Infinitude.

560. Sunishchala: *The Motionless*

ॐ सुनिश्चलाय नमः

Firm and motionless as the mountains, He is stable.

561. Kapila: *Brown*

ॐ कपिलाय नमः

Lord Shiva, the fair-complexioned, the red-lipped, the long-armed Lord, is brown, which denotes that He is without attributes.

562. Kapisha: *Golden*

ॐ कपिशाय नमः

Lord Shiva, golden-hued, is ever radiant.

563. Shukla: *White*

ॐ शुक्लाय नमः

He is an embodiment of all colours that merge to form white, signifying purity.

564. Ayu: *Life Period*

ॐ आयुषे नमः

He is Pure Existence who is deathless.

565. Para: *The Ancient*

ॐ पराय नमः

He is the Oldest of the old.

566. Apara: *The New*

ॐ अपराय नमः

Lord Shiva, the Ageless, is the Oldest of the old, and the Youngest of the young.

567. Gandharva: *The Celestial*

ॐ गन्धर्वाय नमः

He is the Celestial who manifests to attract devotees.

568. Aditi: *The Mother Of Gods*

ॐ अदितये नमः

He is the Earth, the Mother of gods.

569. Tarkshya: *Garuda*

ॐ ताक्ष्याय नमः

He is Garuda, the Prince among birds.

570. Suvijneya: *Known Easily*

ॐ सुविज्ञेयाय नमः

Lord Shiva, the Self, is ever easily known to the self.

571. Susharada: *Of Beautiful Speech*

ॐ सुशारदाय नमः

He is the Lucid Speech, enchanting His audience of devotees.

572. Parashwadhayudha: *Armed With An Axe*

ॐ परश्वधायुधाय नमः

He is armed with the divine axe, Parashwadha.

573. Deva: *Desirous Of Victory*

ॐ देवाय नमः

Lord Shiva, the Deathless, is Victory Personified.

574. Anukari: *Helper In Accomplishment Of Desires*

ॐ अनुकारिणे नमः

He helps others in accomplishing their designs and desires.

575. Subandhava: *A Good Friend*

ॐ सुबान्धवाय नमः

He is the good Friend who helped Arjuna.

576. Tumbaveena: *The Veena*

ॐ तुम्बवीणाय नमः

He is the Veena from whom divine music flows.

577. Mahakrodha: *Of Terrible Anger*

ॐ महाक्रोधाय नमः

He becomes terribly angry during the great deluge.

578. Urdhwareta: *With Progeny Exceeding The Devas*

ॐ ऊर्ध्वरेतसे नमः

He is the Preceptor of Ganesha and Kartikeya who are superior to the gods.

579. Jaleshaya: *Reposing On Water*

ॐ जलेशयाय नमः

He is Vishnu, reposing on the serpent Sesha on water.

580. Ugra: *Swallower With Fierceness*

ॐ उग्राय नमः

He swallows everything with great hunger and ferocity.

581. Vamshakara: *The Attractor*

ॐ वंशकराय नमः

He is the Undisputed Winner over all, attracting everyone by His purity.

582. Vamsha: *The Flute*

ॐ वंशाय नमः

He is the Divine Flute whose melodious notes produce bliss.

583. Vamshanada: *Strains Of The Flute*

ॐ वंशनादाय नमः

He is the melodious strains of the divine flute that tug at the heart-strings.

584. Anindita: *The Faultless*

ॐ अनिन्दिताय नमः

He is Pure Existence, beyond faults, and perfect in everything He does.

585. Sarvangarupa: *Beautiful In All His Limbs*

ॐ सर्वांगरुपाय नमः

He has limbs that are beautiful and beyond comparison, adding to His beauty.

586. Mayavi: *The Producer Of Illusions*

ॐ मायाविने नमः

He is the great Weaver of illusion, and the Lord of nature which is illusion.

587. Suhrida: *The Friend*

ॐ सुहृदाय नमः

He is the Good-hearted Friend who renders help without expectations.

588. Anila: *The Air*

ॐ अनिलाय नमः

He is the Pure Air that one breathes in, dwelling in each as pure Breath.

589. Anala: *The Fire*

ॐ अनलाय नमः

He is the Fire that destroys evil.

590. Bandhana: *The Bond*

ॐ बन्धनाय नमः

He is the Bond that binds the *Jivas*.

591. Bandhakarta: *The Creator Of Bond*

ॐ बन्धकर्त्रे नमः

Bondage has its source in Him.

592. Subandhanavimochana: *The Breaker Of The Bonds*

ॐ सुबन्धनविमोचनाय नमः

He is the happy Breaker of the bonds of *maya* that are very strong.

593. Sayajnari: *The Dweller With The Despoilers Of Sacrifice*

ॐ सयज्ञानारये नमः

He dwells with the despoilers of the sacrifice, standing out as the Supreme.

594. Sakamari: *The Resider With Yogis*

ॐ सकामारये नमः

He dwells with yogis who are conquerors of lust.

595. Mahadamshtra: *The Great Tusk*

ॐ महादंष्ट्राय नमः

He is the Great Tusk that squashes evil.

596. Mahayudha: *Of Mighty Weapons*

ॐ महायुधाय नमः

He possesses mighty divine weapons.

597. Bahudhanindita: *Variously Abused*

ॐ बहुधनिन्दिताय नमः

When He went bare-bodied to Daruka forest, He was abused by sages in many defaming ways.

598. Sharva: *The Fascinator Of The Daruka Sages*

ॐ शर्वाय नमः

He is Sharva who fascinated the sages of the Daruka forest.

599. Shankara: *The Doer Of Good*

ॐ शंकराय नमः

He does good through tormentation.

600. Shankara: *The Destroyer Of All Doubts*

ॐ शंकराय नमः

He destroyed the doubts of the sages, who abused Him, by imparting to them the knowledge of Truth.

601. Adhana: *The Poor*

ॐ अधनाय नमः

He is the Poor, as He is naked, thereby signifying detachment from attachment.

602. Amaresha: *The Lord Of The Gods*

ॐ अमरेशाय नमः

He is Mahadeva, the Lord of the gods.

603. Mahadeva: *Worshipped Even By The Gods*

ॐ महादेवाय नमः

Since the Great One is worshipped by all the gods, He is Mahadeva, *maha* signifying worship.

604. Vishwadeva: *Adored By Vishnu*

ॐ विश्वदेवाय नमः

He is adored by Vishnu, whose name is Vishwa.

605. Surariha: *The Slayer Of The Foes Of Gods*

ॐ सुरारिघ्ने नमः

He slays the enemies who torment the gods.

606. Ahirbudhnya: *As Adisesha Residing In the Netherworld*

ॐ अहिर्बुध्न्याय नमः

He resides as Adisesha, underneath the mundane Egg in the netherworld.

607. Anilabha: *Imperceptible Like The Wind*

ॐ अनिलाभाय नमः

Just as the invisible air is perceived through touch, He is realised through the senses.

608. Chekitana: *Gifted With A Sharp Intellect*

ॐ चेकितानाय नमः

He is gifted with extraordinary powers of perception, perceiving every detail at once.

79

609. Havi: *The Offering*

ॐ हविषे नमः

He is the Offering enjoyed by the consumer.

610. Ajaikapad: *One Of The Eleven Rudras*

ॐ अजैकपादाय नमः

Being one-footed, as in the dance pose, He is Immovable. This is symbolic of Reality being immobile.

611. Kapali: *The Lord Of The Mundane*

ॐ कापालिने नमः

Two halves of the human skull put together form a shell like that of an egg, the two halves representing heaven and earth. This shell contains the entire universe of which He is the Lord.

612. Trishanku: *The Three Gunas*

ॐ त्रिशंकवे नमः

He is the Lord of all lives which along with the world are all within the realm of the three *gunas—sattva, rajas* and *tamas*.

613. Ajita: *The Invincible*

ॐ अजिताय नमः

He cannot be conquered by the three *gunas*.

614. Shiva: *The Pure*

ॐ शिवाय नमः

Purity is the natural state of Lord Shiva, for He is free from limitations.

615. Dhanvantari: *The Great Physician*

ॐ धन्वन्तरये नमः

Lord Shiva, the Great Healer, is the most excellent Physician of all physicians.

616. Dhumaketu: *The Comet*

ॐ धूमकेतवे नमः

He is the comet Dhumaketu, signifying that natural phenomenon belongs to Him.

617. Skanda: *Lord Kartikeya*

ॐ स्कन्दाय नमः

Lord Shiva, the Preceptor of Lord Kartikeya, is the Commander of the forces that are always victorious.

618. Vaishravana: *Kubera*

ॐ वैश्रवणाय नमः

He is Kubera, the Lord of wealth.

619. Dhata: *The Creator Brahma*

ॐ धात्रे नमः

He is Brahma the Creator, as He is also the Sustainer and the Destroyer — He is the Almighty One.

620. Shakra: *Indra*

ॐ शक्राय नमः

He is Indra or Devendra, the Lord of the gods.

621. Vishnu: *The All-pervading One*

ॐ विष्णवे नमः

Lord Shiva, the Creator, the Preserver and the Destroyer, is Vishnu, the All-pervading One.

622. Mitra: *The Sun*

ॐ मित्राय नमः

Lord Shiva, like the Sun, is the Friend of all.

623. Tvashtta: *The Celestial Architect*

ॐ त्वष्टात्रे नमः

He is the Celestial Architect to have fashioned the worlds.

624. Dhruva: *The Pole Star*

ॐ धुवाय नमः

Lord Shiva, like Dhruva the Pole Star, is constant.

625. Dhara: *The Supporter*

ॐ धराय नमः

Lord Shiva, who creates and destroys, also supports everything.

626. Prabhava: *The Origin*

ॐ प्रभावाय नमः

He is the Source, the Origin of everything.

627. Sarvagovayu: *The All-permeating Wind*

ॐ सर्वगोवायवे नमः

He is like Vayu, the wind god, who holds together the world like a thread.

628. Aryama: *A Bosom Friend*

ॐ अर्यमाने नमः

Lord Shiva, a Bosom Friend to His devotees, is the Chief of the *manes*, the sun god.

629. Savita: *The Creator Of Everything*

ॐ सवित्रे नमः

Lord Shiva, the Origin of everything, is the Divine Creator.

630. Ravi: *The Sun*

ॐ रवये नमः

He is radiant and bright like the Sun.

631. Ushangu: *Of Fiery Rays*

ॐ उषंगवे नमः

Lord Shiva, the Soul of everything, is the One with scorching rays.

632. Vidhata: *The Accomplisher*

ॐ विधात्रे नमः

He is the Accomplisher of everything, and Protector in many ways.

633. Mandhata: *The Protector Of Living Beings*

ॐ मान्धात्रे नमः

He is the Protector of the *Jivas*.

634. Bhutabhavana: *The Creator Of The Living Beings*

ॐ भूतभावनाय नमः

He appears as the Self in all, and is the Creator of the living beings.

82

635. Vibhu: *The Omnipresent*

ॐ विभवे नमः

Lord Shiva, the Omnipresent, manifests in several forms.

636. Varnavibhavi: *The Creator Of Colours*

ॐ वर्णविभाविने नमः

Lord Shiva, the Creator of colours, is Himself colourless and without attributes.

637. Sarvakamagunavaha: *Conferring Desires And Attributes*

ॐ सर्वकामगुणावहाय नमः

He enables the devotees to acquire all desirable objects and attributes.

638. Padmanabha: *The Lotus-navelled*

ॐ पद्मनाभाय नमः

He holds the lotus, the abode of the universe, in His navel.

639. Mahagarbha: *The Womb Of The Universe*

ॐ महागर्भाय नमः

He possesses a mighty womb that contains the universe and such great Beings as Brahma.

640. Chandravaktra: *Moon-faced*

ॐ चन्द्रवक्त्राय नमः

His face is as beautiful as the moon.

641. Anila: *The Air*

ॐ अनिलाय नमः

Lord Shiva, the Self-reliant and Self-existent Lord, is the Pure Air that sustains life.

642. Anala: *The Fire*

ॐ अनलाय नमः

Lord Shiva, like the fire, has His power ever on the increase.

643. Balavan: *The Strong*

ॐ बलवते नमः

He is known for His divine strength and power.

644. Upashanta: *Pleasingly Calm*

ॐ उपशान्ताय नमः

Lord Shiva, the most bountiful and compassionate Deity, is always pleasingly calm.

645. Purana: *The Ancient*

ॐ पुराणाय नमः

He is the Oldest of the old, and none existed before Him.

646. Punyachanchuri: *One Who Is Cognised Through Virtue*

ॐ पुण्यचंचवे नमः

He can be realised only by right conduct and practice of virtuous deeds.

647. Aiy: *Lakshmi*

ॐ ऐयाय नमः

He manifests in the form of Lakshmi.

648. Kurukarta: *The Creator Of Kurukshetra*

ॐ करुकर्त्रे नमः

He creates Kurukshetra where acts performed become meritorious.

649. Kuruvasi: *The Dweller In Kurukshetra*

ॐ कुरुवासिने नमः

He dwells in Kurukshetra where His presence effects meritorious acts.

650. Kurubhuta: *The Soul Of Kurukshetra*

ॐ कुरुभूताय नमः

He is the Soul of the field of action to establish righteousness.

651. Gunaushadha: *The Nurturer Of Virtues*

ॐ गुणोषधाय नमः

He nurtures attributes such as wealth, knowledge, dispassion and *dharma*.

84

652. Sarvashaya: *The Resting Place Of All Beings*

ॐ सर्वाशयाय नमः

In sound sleep all beings merge in the Lord, and hence He is the Abode of all.

653. Darbhachari: *Consumer Of Offerings On Darbha Grass*

ॐ दर्भचारिणे नमः

He accepts the sacrificial offerings placed on the sacred darbha grass.

654. Sarvesham Praninampati: *The Lord Of All Beings*

ॐ सर्वेषां प्राणिनांपतये नमः

Lord Shiva, the Creator of the worlds, is the Lord of all beings.

655. Devadeva: *The God Of Gods*

ॐ देवदेवाय नमः

He is the Almighty One, who is the God of the gods.

656. Sukhasakta: *Unattached To Pleasures*

ॐ सुखासक्ताय नमः

He is detached from all pleasures.

657. Sat: *The Reality*

ॐ सते नमः

He is the Absolute Reality who causes effect.

658. Asat: *The Phenomenal Reality*

ॐ असते नमः

He is the Phenomenal Reality, creating cause and effect.

659. Sarvaratnavit: *Possessor Of All Earthly Wealth*

ॐ सर्वरत्नविदे नमः

He is the Owner of all precious earthly wealth.

660. Kailasagirivasi: *Resider In The Kailasa*

ॐ कैलासगिरिवासिने नमः

He makes Mount Kailasa as His abode.

661. Himavatgirisamshraya: *Dweller In The Himalayas*
ॐ हिमवत्गिरिसंश्रयाय नमः
The Great Lord, fond of the mountains, dwells in the Himalayas.

662. Kulahari: *The Destroyer Of River Banks*
ॐ कूलहारिणे नमः
Like floods which destroy trees on the banks of rivers, He destroys the river banks.

663. Kulakarta: *The Fashioner Of Lakes*
ॐ कूलकर्त्रे नमः
He is the Creator of lakes such as the Pushkara.

664. Bahuvidya: *The Omniscient*
ॐ बहुविद्याय नमः
Lord Shiva, the Omniscient, is cognizant of the various sciences.

665. Bahuprada: *The Munificent Giver*
ॐ बहुप्रदाय नमः
He confers many things on the virtuous.

666. Vanija: *The Merchant*
ॐ वणिजाय नमः
Like the merchant, He deals with beings successfully.

667. Vardhaki: *The Carpenter*
ॐ वर्धकिने नमः
He is the Creator who has fashioned the universe.

668. Vruksha: *The Tree*
ॐ वृक्षाय नमः
He is the Great Tree providing shelter to the seekers.

669. Vakula: *Vakula Tree*
ॐ वकुलाय नमः
He is the Vakula Tree under which a devotee seeks knowledge.

86

670. Chandana: *The Sandal Tree*

ॐ चन्दनाय नमः

He is the Sandal Tree whose perfume pervades space.

671. Chhada: *The Seven-leaved Tree*

ॐ श्री छदाय नमः

Lord Shiva is the seven-leaved Tree that provides nourishment to the righteous.

672. Saragriva: *The Mighty-necked*

ॐ सारग्रीवाय नमः

His mighty neck consumed the venomous poison that nearly destroyed the populace.

673. Mahajatru: *Of Mighty Collar Bones*

ॐ महाजत्रवे नमः

He has mighty collar bones that support strong shoulders.

674. Alola: *Steady*

ॐ अलोलाय नमः

He is imbued with steadiness.

675. Mahaushadha: *Manifests As Foodgrains*

ॐ महौषधाय नमः

Lord Shiva, the Great Sustainer, manifests as foodgrains.

676. Siddharthakari: *The Accomplisher Of Desires*

ॐ सिद्धार्थकारिणे नमः

He grants success to the devotees in their undertakings to accomplish their objectives.

677. Siddharthashchhando Vyakaranottara: *Adept In Scripture Lore*

ॐ श्री सिद्धार्थश्छन्दो व्याकरणोत्तराय नमः

He is adept in the grammar and scriptures accompanied by their commentaries.

678. Simhanada: *With Leonine Roar*

ॐ सिंहनादाय नमः

Lord Shiva, the Creator of sound, can roar like a lion.

679. Simhadamshtra: *Lion-fanged*

ॐ सिंहदंष्ट्राय नमः

Lord Shiva, in His terrible manifestation, has fangs like the lion.

680. Simhaga: *The Lion-rider*

ॐ सिंहगाय नमः

Lord Shiva and Goddess Parvati ride the lion and the bull.

681. Simhavahana: *He Whose Vehicle Is A Lion*

ॐ सिंहवाहनाय नमः

Lord Shiva, apart from using the bull as His vehicle, also rides the lion.

682. Prabhavatma: *The Truth Of Truths*

ॐ प्रभावात्मने नमः

The senses are truth and Lord Shiva is their Truth.

683. Jagatkalasthala: *The Devourer Of The Universe*

ॐ जगत्कालस्थालाय नमः

Lord Shiva, during the dissolution, swallows the universe.

684. Lokahita: *The Benefactor Of The World*

ॐ लोकहिताय नमः

Lord Shiva, being the Benefactor of the world, is much revered and adored.

685. Taru: *The Saviour*

ॐ तरवे नमः

He saves beings from straying waywardly.

686. Saranga: *The Bird Saranga*

ॐ सारंगाय नमः

Lord Shiva, in one of His manifestations, is the Saranga bird.

687. Navachakranga: *The New Swan*

ॐ नवचक्रांगाय नमः

The Swan indicates the Almighty who is ever new.

688. Ketumali: *With a Shining Crest*

ॐ श्री केतुमालिने नमः

His beauty is enhanced by a shining crest like that of a peacock.

689. Sabhavana: *The Head Of A Council*

ॐ सभावानाय नमः

He is the Protector of the places of justice, being the Head of all.

690. Bhutalaya: *The Abode Of Beings*

ॐ भूतालयाय नमः

Lord Shiva, the Protector and Sustainer, is the Abode of all beings.

691. Bhutapati: *The Lord Of Beings*

ॐ भूतपतये नमः

Lord Shiva, the Creator and the Almighty, is the Lord of all beings.

692. Ahoratra: *Day And Night*

ॐ अहोरात्राय नमः

Lord Shiva, the Controller of time, is the eternal day-night circle.

693. Anindita: *The Faultless*

ॐ अनिन्दिताय नमः

He is faultless, being Pure Existence.

694. Vahitasarvabhutanam: *The Bearer Of All Beings*

ॐ वाहिता सर्वभूतानाम् वाहित्रे नमः

Lord Shiva, being magnanimous and most considerate, is the Bearer of all beings.

695. Nilaya: *The Dwelling Place Of Beings*

ॐ निलयाय नमः

He is the Abode where all beings reside.

696. Vibhu: *The Unborn*

ॐ विभवे नमः

Lord Shiva, the Unborn, has no beginning or end.

697. Bhava: *Become*

ॐ भवाय नमः

He is the Cause of the manifestation of all beings.

698. Amogha: *Fruitful*

ॐ अमोघाय नमः

He is the Accomplisher of everything, being fruitful in all He does.

699. Samyata: *Concentrated*

ॐ सम्यताय नमः

He is endowed with complete concentration.

700. Ashwa: *The Horse*

ॐ अश्वाय नमः

He is the Divine Horse fulfilling desires.

701. Bhojana: *The Giver Of Food*

ॐ भोजनाय नमः

The Most Bountiful Lord is the Giver of food.

702. Prandharana: *The Protector Of Life*

ॐ प्राणधारणाय नमः

The Almighty Lord is the Protector of all lives.

703. Dhritiman: *Imbued With Fortitude*

ॐ धृतिमते नमः

The Lord of all beings is endowed with limitless fortitude.

704. Matiman: *The Highly Intelligent*

ॐ मतिमते नमः

The highly Intelligent Lord Shiva is the great fount and storehouse of limitless knowledge.

705. Daksha: *The Clever*

ॐ दक्षाय नमः

The supremely Wise Lord Shiva is clever and persevering.

706. Satkruta: *Revered By All*

ॐ सत्कृताय नमः

The Omniscient and Omnipotent Lord Shiva is revered and respected by all.

707. Yugadhipa: *The Lord Of The Yugas*

ॐ युगाधिपाय नमः

He dispenses the fruits of virtue and vice.

708. Gopala: *The Protector Of The Senses*

ॐ गोपालाय नमः

The highly Intelligent Lord Shiva is the Lord of the senses which He protects.

709. Gopati: *The Lord Of The Luminaries*

ॐ गोपतये नमः

He is the Lord of the rays of luminaries like the sun.

710. Grama: *Group*

ॐ ग्रामाय नमः

He is the Lord of all groups—people, celestials, sages, etc.

711. Gocharmavasana: *Draped With Cowhides*

ॐ गोचर्मवसनाय नमः

Lord Shiva, the Great Ascetic, drapes Himself with the hide of the cow.

712. Hari: *The Destroyer*

ॐ हरये नमः

He is the Destroyer of the sorrows of His devotees.

713. Hiranyabahu: *Of Beautiful Arms*

ॐ हिरण्यबाहवे नमः

Lord Shiva, the handsome, strong and noble Ruler, is endowed with beautiful arms.

714. Praveshinam Guhapala: *The Protector Of Yogis' Bodies*

ॐ प्रवेशिनां गुहापालाय नमः

When the bodies of yogis go into *samadhi*, He protects these bodies.

715. Prakrushtari: *The Vanquisher Of Inner Foes*

ॐ प्रकृष्टारये नमः

He vanquishes the desires, lust, greed, etc., of the advanced aspirants.

616. Mahaharsha: *One In Ecstasy*

ॐ महाहर्षाय नमः

Lord Shiva, always in ecstasy, is Pure Bliss.

617. Jitakama: *The Subduer Of Lust*

ॐ जितकामाय नमः

He subdues lust and conquers love.

718. Jitendriya: *The Subjugator Of The Senses*

ॐ जितेन्द्रियाय नमः

He who controls the senses, subjugates them at will.

719. Gandhara: *The Musical Note 'Mi'*

ॐ गान्धाराय नमः

Lord Shiva, the Creator of sound, is the musical note *Mi* in the gamut of music.

720. Suvasa: *The Resident Of Kailasa*

ॐ सुवासाय नमः

He possesses a fine dwelling place — Mount Kailasha.

721. Tapassakta: *Immersed In Penance*

ॐ तपस्सक्ताय नमः

He is the Great Ascetic who immerses in penance and is devoted to meditation.

722. Rati: *The Indulger*

ॐ रतये नमः

He indulges in joy; He is Pure Bliss.

723. Nara: *The Cosmic Deity Virat*

॰ॐ नराय नमः

He is the cosmic deity Virat who rules the mundane Egg.

724. Mahageeta: *The Ardent Lover Of Music*

ॐ महागीताय नमः

The Creator of sound, Lord Shiva, is a great Patron of music.

725. Mahanrutya: *The Delighter In Dance*

ॐ महानृत्याय नमः

As the king of all dances, He delights in dancing the *Thandava* and the *Lasya* dances.

726. Apsaroganasevita: *Worshipped By Bands Of Celestials*

ॐ अप्सरोगसेविताय नमः

Lord Shiva, the Adorable One, is worshipped by hordes of *apsaras*.

727. Mahaketu: *Mighty-bannered*

ॐ महाकेतवे नमः

He possesses the significant standard with the insignia of the bull.

728. Mahadhatu: *Mount Meru*

ॐ महाधात्रे नमः

He is Mount Meru which is the abode of many.

729. Naikasanuchara: *The Wanderer Over The Mountains*

ॐ नैकसानुचराय नमः

He wanders over the summits of many mountains.

730. Chala: *Ever-moving*

ॐ चलाय नमः

He is too mobile to be ever caught.

731. Avedaniya: *Cognisable*

ॐ आवेदनीयाय नमः

Lord Shiva, though transcending speech, could be explained by teachers so as to be cognisable.

732. Adesha: *Instruction*

ॐ आदेशाय नमः

He is the Instruction or Teaching that a pupil receives joyfully.

733. Sarvagandhasukhavaha: *The Producer Of The Pleasure Through Fragrances*

ॐ सर्वगन्धसुखावहाय नमः

Lord Shiva, who is Pure Bliss, produces pleasure through fragrances.

734. Torana: *The Decorated Doorway*

ॐ तोरणाय नमः

He is the Ornate Arch and Doorway of entrances.

735. Tarana: *One Who Wards Off Difficulties*

ॐ तारणाय नमः

He enables one to ward off missiles of difficulties.

736. Vata: *The Wind*

ॐ वाताय नमः

Lord Shiva, eternally moving, is the Wind that creates movement.

737. Paridhi: *The Fortress*

ॐ परिधिने नमः

He is the Impregnable Fortress, providing protection to the deserving.

738. Patikhechara: *Garuda*

ॐ पतिखेचराय नमः

He is the Lord of birds, Garuda, who protects the hapless.

739. Samyogovardhana: *The Fruitful Union*

ॐ संयोगोवर्धनाय नमः

All acts have their due place in the functioning of the cosmos, and He is the fruitful Union between the sexes.

94

740. Vrudha: *The Old*

ॐ वृद्धाय नमः

He is the Oldest in knowledge and experience, which counts for everything.

741. Ativrudha: *The Very Old*

ॐ अतिवृद्धाय नमः

He is the Oldest of the old.

742. Gunadhika: *One Who Excels In Character*

ॐ गुणाधिकाय नमः

He excels in His good attributes.

743. Nityamatmasahaya: *The Eternal Help Of Living Beings*

ॐ नित्यमात्मसहायाय नमः

He is extremely magnanimous and eternally helpful to all living beings.

744. Devasurapati: *The Lord Of The Gods And Demons*

ॐ देवासुरपतये नमः

Lord Shiva, the Ruler of all, is the Lord of the gods and the demons.

745. Pati: *The Ruler Of All*

ॐ पतये नमः

He is the Ruler of all living beings.

746. Yukta: *Ready For Fight*

ॐ युक्ताय नमः

Lord Shiva, the strong-armed Deity, is ever prepared to fight, and yet united with all.

747. Yuktabahu: *With Arms Ever Ready For Action*

ॐ युक्ताबाहवे नमः

He has strong arms, powerful enough to quell His foes.

748. Divisuparvanodeva: *Worshipped By Indra In Heaven*

ॐ दिविसुपर्वणोदेवाय नमः

The Reverent and Adorable Shiva is worshipped by Indra in Heaven.

749. Ashaddha: *Enabling One To Bear Everything*

ॐ आषाढ़ाय नमः

He provides the devotees the power of endurance.

750. Sushaddha: *Equipped With Endurance*

ॐ सुषाढ़ाय नमः

He confers the power of endurance on His devotees in a limited way.

751. Dhruva: *The Motionless*

ॐ धुवाय नमः

Lord Shiva, who creates movement, is motionless.

752. Harina: *The Pure White*

ॐ हरिणाय नमः

He is pure white, signifying Pure Existence.

753. Hara: *The Destroyer Of Misery*

ॐ हराय नमः

Armed with the trident, Lord Shiva destroys all miseries.

754. Avartamanebhyovapu: *The Granter Of Bodies*

ॐ आवर्तमानेभ्योवपुशे नमः

Those who take birth are granted bodies by Lord Shiva.

755. Vasushreshttha: *Greater Than Wealth*

ॐ वसुश्रेठाय नमः

Lord Shiva, who is dearer and greater than wealth, is the greatest wealth.

756. Mahapata: *The Great Path*

ॐ महापताय नमः

He is the Great Path which is the rule of life of the holy ones.

757. Shirohari-Vimarsha: *He Who Removed Brahma's Head After Consideration*

ॐ शिरोहारी – विमर्शाय नमः

Lord Shiva is said to have chipped off Brahma's head, not in anger but after due consideration — a mythical story indicating the appropriateness of adding or reducing the limbs of the deities.

758. Sarvalakshanalakshita: *Endowed With Auspicious Marks*

ॐ सर्वलक्षणलक्षिताय नमः

Lord Shiva, with a classical body, bears all auspicious marks, but is difficult to be realised.

759. Akshara-Rathayogi: *The Axle Of The Chariot*

ॐ अक्षाय रथयोगिने नमः

He is the Axle of the chariot of the universe.

760. Sarvayogi: *Linked With All*

ॐ सर्वयोगिने नमः

He is linked with everything — nothing exists independently.

761. Mahabala: *The Mightiest*

ॐ महाबलाय नमः

He is the mightiest and most valiant of the Deities.

762. Samamnaya: *The Vedas*

ॐ समाम्नायाय नमः

Lord Shiva, the limitless Fount of knowledge, is the essence of the *Vedas*.

763. Asamamnaya: *Transcending The Vedas*

ॐ असमाम्नायाय नमः

He transcends the *Vedas* and other scriptures like the *Puranas*, the Agamas the *Itihasas*.

764. Teerthhadeva: *The Lord Of Holy Places*

ॐ तीर्थदेवाय नमः

He is the Lord of all the holy places visited by His devotees.

765. Maharatha: *The Great Chariot*

ॐ महारथाय नमः

He is the Great Chariot comprising all the moving planets.

766. Nirjeeva: *The Insentient*

ॐ निर्जीवाय नमः

He is the Soul of the material world.

767. Jivana: *The Conferrer Of Life*

ॐ जीवनाय नमः

He is the Awakener of Life in the seeming lifeless.

768. Mantra: *Pranava And Other Sacred Formulas*

ॐ मन्त्राय नमः

He is that Sound which infuses life or additional *mantra* — He is the *pranava* and the other sacred formulas.

769. Shubhaksha: *Of Calm Looks*

ॐ शुभाक्षाय नमः

He has a gracious glance and wears a calm look on His face.

770. Bahukarkasha: *The Stern Disciplinarian*

ॐ बहुकर्कशाय नमः

He can be soft as well as stern as the situation demands.

771. Ratnaprabhuta: *With Gem-like Qualities*

ॐ रत्नप्रभूताय नमः

He is most virtuous and has gem-like pure qualities.

772. Raktanga: *The Red-bodied*

ॐ रक्तांगाय नमः

He is very handsome with a fair-complexioned face and a red body.

773. Maharnavanipanavit: *The Consumer Of The Oceans*

ॐ महार्णवनिपानविदे नमः

He swallows the oceans while in dissolution.

774. Moolan: *The Root Of The Family Tree*

ॐ मूलाय नमः

He is the Root Cause of the phenomenon—the root that supports the *Samsara* tree.

775. Vishala: *The Illustrious*

ॐ विशालाय नमः

He is the Wise One, the Illustrious and Radiant Almighty.

776. Amruta: *The Ambrosia*

ॐ अमृताय नमः

He is the Ambrosia that is Pure Bliss.

777. Vyakthavyatha: *The Manifest And The Unmanifest*

ॐ व्यक्ताव्यक्ताय नमः

He is the Manifest and the Unmanifest; with and without attributes.

778. Taponidhi: *The Storehouse Of Austerities*

ॐ तपोनिधये नमः

He is the excellent Treasure of austerities, being the Great Ascetic that He is.

779. Arohana: *The Steps To Godhood*

ॐ आरोहय नमः

He is the Steps that lead the aspirants to the Supreme.

780. Adhiroha: *The One Seated In Godhood*

ॐ अधिरोहाय नमः

He is the Ultimate Goal that aspirants try to reach.

781. Sheeladhari: *The Possessor Of Virtues*

ॐ शीलधारिणे नमः

Lord Shiva, possessing divine virtues, is of noble conduct.

782. Mahayasha: *The Abode Of Fame*

ॐ महायशसे नमः

He is of pure renown and the Abode of fame.

783. Senakalpa: *The Animator Of The Army*

ॐ सेनाकल्पाय नमः

He is the *Ornament* of the army, known for His valour and competence.

784. Mahakalpa: *The Mightily Competent*

ॐ महाकल्पाय नमः

Lord Shiva, with divine ornaments, is beyond defeat and death, and is extremely competent.

785. Yoga: *The Seat Of Yoga*

ॐ योगाय नमः

He is the Seat of Yoga, restraining the functions of the mind.

786. Yugakara: *The Embodiment Of Time In The Yugas*

ॐ युगकराय नमः

He embodies time as indicated in the *yugas*.

787. Hari: *Vishnu*

ॐ हरये नमः

He is also Vishnu, for He is the Trinity.

788. Yugarupa: *The Time Factor*

ॐ युगरूपाय नमः

He is the Time factor blending past and present, vice and virtue.

789. Maharupa: *The Imperceptibly Formless*

ॐ महारूपाय नमः

He is both formless and of beautiful form, difficult to be realised.

790. Mahanagahana: *The Slayer Of The Great Elephant*

ॐ महानागहनाय नमः

He is the Slayer of Gajasura, the demon in the form of an elephant.

791. Vadha: *Death*

ॐ वधाय नमः

He is Death of the evil forces.

792. Nyayanirvapana: *Justly Charitable*

ॐ न्यायनिर्वपणाय नमः

He is the Distributor of justice according to one's just dessert.

793. Pada: *The Goal*

ॐ पादाय नमः

He is the Goal to be attained.

794. Pandita: *The Learned*

ॐ पण्डिताय नमः

He is the Learned, the Divine Scholar who realises things indirectly.

795. Achalopama: *The Motionless*

ॐ अचलोपमाय नमः

Lord Shiva, creating movements, is immobile, the Realiser of Truth.

796. Bahumala: *Of Infinite Manifestations*

ॐ बहुमालाय नमः

When He manifests, each time He takes a different form.

797. Mahamala: *The Profusely Garlanded*

ॐ महामालाय नमः

He wears garlands that hang down to touch His feet.

798. Shashi-Harasulochana: *Moon-like Calm-eyed*

ॐ शशिने हरसुलोचनाय नमः

He has eyes that are lustrous and calm like the moon.

799. Vistara-Lavana Kupa: *The Vast Ocean*

ॐ विस्ताराय लवणाय कूपाय नमः

He is the Vast Ocean which is His water-tank.

800. Triyuga: *The First Three Yugas*

ॐ त्रियुगाय नमः

He is the first three Yugas, which does not include the Kaliyuga.

801. Safalodaya: *With Fruitful Results*

ॐ सफलोदयाय नमः

His appearance is fruitful and everything He accomplishes with fruitful results.

802. Trilochana: *The Three-eyed*

ॐ त्रिलोचनाय नमः

His third eye is one of intuition.

803. Vishannanga: *Endowed With Eight Forms*

ॐ विषण्णांगाय नमः

He is endowed with eight forms, such as the Earth, etc., which, though formless, are related to Him in their subtle aspect — He is their Inner Soul.

804. Manividdha: *With Ears Pierced For Earrings*

ॐ मणिविद्धाय नमः

He has His ears pierced, for wearing earrings.

805. Jatadhara: *Wearing Matted Hair*

ॐ जटाधराय नमः

Lord Shiva, with His matted hair, sports the river Ganga on His tendrils.

806. Bindu: *The Dot Representing Anuswara*

ॐ बिन्दवे नमः

He is the Divine Dot representing the first notes of music.

807. Visarga: *Constantly Moving*

ॐ विसर्गाय नमः

Lord Shiva, the Creator of movement, is rooted, yet moving.

808. Sumukha: *The Pleasant-faced*

ॐ सुमुखाय नमः

He is the Pleasant faced Deity with manifested syllables.

809. Shara: *The Arrow*

ॐ शराय नमः

He is the Divine Arrow that finds its target faultlessly.

810. Sarvayudha: *Armed With All Weapons*

ॐ सर्वायुधाय नमः

Lord Shiva, the strong, brave Warrior, is armed with all weapons.

811. Saha: *Calm Endurance*

ॐ सहाय नमः

He has the calmness to endure everything.

812. Nivedana: *The Dedication*

ॐ निवेदनाय नमः

He is Dedication Personified, whose knowledge is free of all modifications.

813. Sukhajata: *One Who Appears As Bliss*

ॐ सुखाजाताय नमः

He is the Bliss following the cessation of the mind.

814. Sugandhara: *Fine Music*

ॐ सुगन्धाराय नमः

Lord Shiva, taking birth in one of His manifestations in the beautiful Gandhara country, is the Melodious Music humming out fine notes.

815. Mahadhanu: *The Mighty Bow*

ॐ महाधनुषे नमः

He bears the mighty bow Pinaka, which is a powerful force of destruction.

816. Gandhapali-Bhagavan: *The Preserver Of Perfumes*

ॐ गन्धपालिने भगवते नमः

Lord Shiva, the Preserver and Maker of perfumes, is the Aggregate of the mental impressions of all beings.

817. Sarvakarmanam-Utthan: *The Source Of All Actions*

ॐ सर्वकर्मणाम उत्थानाय नमः

All actions take root from Him.

818. Manthana Bahula Vayu: *The Great Wind Churning All*

ॐ मन्थानाय बहुल वायवे नमः

He is the Stormy Wind during the deluge that shakes up everything.

819. Sakala: *The Entirety*

ॐ सकलाय नमः

He is perfect in all ways, and He is the Entirety.

820. Sarvalochana: *The Omni-seer*

ॐ सर्वलोचनाय नमः

Lord Shiva, with limitless vision, sees everything, being the All-seeing.

821. Talastala: *Having Cymbals In Hand*

ॐ तलस्ताल नमः

He holds a cymbal in one of His hands.

822. Karasthali: *Using The Palm As A Plate*

ॐ करस्थालिने नमः

He uses His palm instead of a plate for eating.

823. Urdhvasamhanana: *Of Robust Body*

ॐ ऊर्ध्वसंहननाय नमः

His body is well knit and robust.

824. Mahan: *Of Great Personality*

ॐ महते नमः

He has a tall and great personality.

825. Chhatra: *The Umbrella*

ॐ छत्राय नमः

He is the Wide Umbrella, offering shelter to the multitudinous.

826. Suchhatra: *With A Good Umbrella*

ॐ सुछत्राय नमः

He has a good umbrella under which the aspirants seek shelter.

827. Vikhyata-Loka: *Well Known Among People*

ॐ विख्यात – लोकाय नमः

He is well-known among people because His light is perceived only in them.

828. Sarvashraya-Krama: *Whose Footsteps Are The Abode Of Everything*

ॐ सर्वाश्रयायः क्रमाय नमः

Lord Shiva, who measured the three worlds with His steps, is the abode of everything.

829. Munda: *With Shaven Head*

ॐ मुण्डाय नमः

Lord Shiva, with His head shaven, is the Perfect Ascetic.

830. Virupa: *The Uncouth*

ॐ विरूपाय नमः

Lord Shiva, with His head shaven, looks uncouth, but He is detached from all worldly appearances.

831. Vikruta: *The Disfigured*

ॐ विकृताय नमः

Lord Shiva, undergoing all changes, appears disfigured, which is but an illusion.

832. Dandi: *With A Stick*

ॐ दण्डिने नमः

Lord Shiva, as the Divine Ascetic, holds a stick.

833. Kundi: *With A Pot*

ॐ कुण्डिने नमः

The Austere Ascetic holds a pot in His hand, indicating few needs.

834. Vikurvana: *The Unattainable Through Rituals*

ॐ विकुर्वणाय नमः

He can be attained only through the senses and meditation, not mere rituals.

835. Haryaksha: *The Lion*

ॐ हर्यक्षाय नमः

He is the Lion, lordly and noble in demeanor and conduct.

836. Kakubha: *All The Quarters*

ॐ ककुभाय नमः

He is all the quarters of space, all pervading and filling up everything.

837. Vajrine: *The Wielder Of The Thunderbolt*

ॐ वज्रिने नमः

He wields the thunderbolt, called vajra.

838. Shatajihva: *The Hundred-tongued*

ॐ शतजिह्वाय नमः

He is the Hundred-tongued during the dissolution.

839. Sahastrapat: *The Thousand-footed*

ॐ सहस्त्रपादे नमः

The feet of all the beings are His.

840. Sahastramurdha: *The Thousand-headed*

ॐ सहस्त्रमूर्ध्ने नमः

He manifests through all the heads.

841. Devendra-Sarvadevamaya: *Consisting Of All The Gods*

ॐ देवेन्द्राय सर्वदेवमयाय नमः

All the gods have their source in Him.

842. Guru: *The Teacher*

ॐ गुरवे नमः

With a limitless fount of knowledge, He is the Supremely Wise Teacher.

843. Sahastrabahu: *The Thousand-armed*

ॐ सहस्त्रबाहवे नमः

Lord Shiva, attributeless, is thousand-armed when He manifests.

844. Sarvanga: *Possessing Everything*

ॐ सर्वांगाय नमः

Lord Shiva, attaining everything, possesses them all.

845. Sharanya: *The Giver Of Shelter*

ॐ शरण्याय नमः

Lord Shiva, fit to take refuge with, gives shelter to the seekers.

846. Sarvalokakrut: *The Creator Of All The Worlds*

ॐ सर्वलोककृते नमः

He is the Creator of all the worlds which total fourteen.

847. Pavitram: *The Purifier*

ॐ पवित्राय नमः

He is the Purifier of place, making them holy for beings to visit and get purified.

848. Trikakunmantra: *The Mantra Containing Three Essentials*

ॐ त्रिककुन्मन्त्राय नमः

He is the Mantra that constitutes *bija*, *shakti* and *kilakam* — the three essential factors that make the mantra divine.

849. Kanishttha: *The Youngest*

ॐ कनिष्ठाय नमः

He is the youngest of the sons of Aditi-Lord Vishnu as Vamana.

850. Krishnapingala: *Black And Red*

ॐ कृष्णपिंगलाय नमः

Here the colours denote Vishnu and Shiva, respectively — Lord Shiva is both Hara and Hari (Vishnu and Shiva).

851. Brahmadandavinirmata: *The Fashioner Of Brahma's Wand*

ॐ ब्रह्मदण्डविनिर्मात्रे नमः

He is responsible for fashioning the divine wand of Brahma.

852. Shataghni-Pasha-Shaktiman: *Amed With The Nooe And Shakti*

ॐ शतघ्नी पाशशक्तिमते नमः

Lord Shiva, armed with the noose called Shataghni, and Shakti, is capable of killing a hundred at a time.

853. Padmagarbha: *The Lotus-born*

ॐ श्री पद्मगर्भाय नमः

Lord Shiva, who is the Trinity, is Brahma, the lotus-born.

854. Mahagarbha: *The Container Of All*

ॐ महागर्भाय नमः

He is the vast womb with a vast hollow inside, containing all creation.

855. Brahmagarbha: *The Container Of The Vedas*

ॐ ब्रह्मगर्भाय नमः

Lord Shiva, the vast Womb holding all creation, also has the *Vedas* in Him.

856. Jalodbhava: *Born In The Waters*

ॐ जलोद्भवाय नमः

The Master of Maya, Lord Shiva is the Origin of life from water in the new creation.

857. Gabhasti: *Rays Of Refulgent Light*

ॐ गभस्तये नमः

He is radiant like the million suns, which are refulgent with rays.

858. Brahmakrut: *The Author Of The Vedas*

ॐ ब्रह्मकृते नमः

Lord Shiva, with His vast fount of divine knowledge, is the Maker of the *Vedas*.

859. Brahmi: *Reciter Of The Vedas*

ॐ ब्रह्मिणे नमः

Lord Shiva, the Maker of the *Vedas*, is also its Reciter.

860. Brahmavit: *The Knower Of The Vedas*

ॐ ब्रह्मविदे नमः

He is the Author and Reciter of the *Vedas,* and is conversant with the text.

861. Brahmana: *In The Form Of The Brahman*

ॐ ब्राह्मणाय नमः

He is the Brahman, the Supreme One.

862. Gati: *The Goal*

ॐ गतये नमः

He is the Goal of the knowers of the Brahman.

863. Anantarupa: *Of Infinite Forms*

ॐ अनन्तरूपाय नमः

He manifest in various infinite forms.

864. Naikatma: *The Omni-bodied*

ॐ नैकात्माय नमः

He takes various forms in His manifestations.

865. Swayambuva Tigmateja: *Brahma Overwhelmed By Shiva*

ॐ स्वयम्भुवः तिग्मतेजसे नमः

Brahma viewed Lord Shiva to be unbearable prowess and He cut off his head.

866. Urdhvagatma: *The Transcendent Reality*

ॐ ऊर्ध्वगात्मणे नमः

Lord Shiva, having enveloped the Earth all round, stood out ten inches beyond, thereby transcending it.

867. Pashupati: *The Lord Of Beings*

ॐ पशुपतये नमः

Lord Shiva, the Creator and Sustainer, is the Lord of all beings.

868. Vataramha: *Swift As The Wind*

ॐ वातरंहाय नमः

Lord Shiva, the All-pervading, is everywhere at all times as He is swift as the wind.

869. Manojava: *Instantaneous As The Mind*

ॐ मनोजवाय नमः

He is swift and instantaneous like the mind.

870. Chandani: *Smeared With Sandal Paste*

ॐ चन्दनिने नमः

The Great Ascetic is smeared with the fragrant sandal paste.

871. Padmanalagra: *The Immeasured Lotus-born*

ॐ पद्मनालाग्राय नमः

Lord Shiva, who is beyond dimensions, is born from the lotus in one of His manifestations. Lord Brahma, wishing to ascertain the end of the lotus stem wherein he resided, could never see its end.

872. Surabhyutharana: *The Degrader Of Surabhi*

ॐ सुरभ्युत्तरणाय नमः

Surabhi, the cow of plenty, was compelled to tell a lie by Brahma, and was degraded from her high level by Lord Shiva.

873. Nara: *He Who Cannot Find The Terminal*

ॐ नराय नमः

Lord Brahma cannot find either the head or the feet of Lord Shiva, who is immeasurable.

874. Karnikara-Mahasragvi: *Garland With Karnikara Flowers*

ॐ कर्णिकार–महास्रग्विने नमः

Lord Shiva, the Supreme One, wears a garland of *karnikara* flowers.

875. Neelamauli: *Crowned With Blue Gems*

ॐ नीलमौलये नमः

Lord Shiva, sporting matted hair, is crowned with the River Ganga whose water's sparkle like blue gems.

876. Pinakadhrut: *The Wielder Of Pinaka*

ॐ पिनाकधृते नमः

He used the Pinaka, the divine bow, in wresting the heaven for the gods from Tripurasura, the Mount Meru.

877. Umapati: *The Lord Of Uma*

ॐ उमापतये नमः

As the Lord of Uma (or Parvati), He is reverenced with coral tree flowers and other celestial flowers.

878. Umakanta: *Attained By Uma*

ॐ उमाकान्ताय नमः

He is the Embodiment of knowledge which Uma attained.

879. Jahnavidhrut: *The Bearer Of Ganga*

ॐ जाह्नवीधृते नमः

He bears the sacred Ganga on His locks of matted hair.

880. Umadhava: *The Lord Of Uma*

ॐ उमाधवाय नमः

He is the Husband of Uma or Parvati.

881. Varo-Varaha: *The Mighty Boar*

ॐ वराय वराहाय नमः

He regenerated the earth in the shape of the boar called Yajnavaraha.

882. Varada: *The Bestower Of Boons*

ॐ वरदाय नमः

Lord Shiva, who bestows boons, is the Protector of the universe through many divine forms.

883. Varenya: *The Sought-after*

ॐ वरेण्याय नमः

He is most sought after. He is the One competent to offer boons.

884. Sumahaswana: *The Melodious Voice*

ॐ सुमहास्वनाय नमः

He has a Melodious Voice to recite the *Vedas*.

885. Mahaprasada: *Of Great Favour*

ॐ महाप्रसादाय नमः

Lord Shiva, of incomparable grace, is greatly favoured.

886. Damana: *The Subjugator Of The Wicked*

ॐ दमनाय नमः

Lord Shiva, worshipped by death, subjugates the wicked.

887. Shatruha: *The Destroyer Of Foes*

ॐ शत्रुघ्ने नमः

He destroys desires and other internal foes.

888. Shwetapingala: *The White-and-red-coloured*

ॐ श्वेतपिंगलाय नमः

He is the Ardhanari Nateshwara, who is white on His right side and red on His left.

889. Preetatma: *The Golden-hued*

ॐ प्रीतात्मने नमः

He is seen in the body of the sun, with hair of golden hue – golden all over.

890. Paramatma: *The Supreme Atman*

ॐ परमात्मने नमः

He transcends the five forms of Atman and is Absolute Bliss.

891. Prayatatma: *The Pure-minded*

ॐ प्रयतात्मने नमः

He is pure-minded, and hence Pure Bliss.

892. Pradhanadhrut: *The Foundation Of The Phenomenon*

ॐ प्रधानधृते नमः

He presides over ignorance, producing the three *gunas* that form the cause of the universe.

893. Sarvaparshwamukha: *The All-sides-faced*

ॐ सर्वपार्श्वमुखाय नमः

He faces on all sides — in the four quarters and above.

894. Trayaksha: *The Three-eyed*

ॐ त्र्यक्षाय नमः

He has three eyes represented by the moon, the sun and the fire.

895. Dharmasadharanavara: *Favourable According to The Virtues*

ॐ धर्मसाधारणोवराय नमः

He is favourable according to the virtues of His devotees — as one deserves, so one gets.

896. Characharatma: *The Soul Of The Two Paths*

ॐ चराचरात्मने नमः

He is the Two Paths — the fixed and the changing — attained through merit and grace.

897. Sukshmatma: *The Subtle Self*

ॐ सूक्षात्मने नमः

He is too subtle for one to easily attain the heavenly paths.

898. Amruta-Govrusheshwara: *Devoid Of Death*

ॐ अमृताय – गोवृषेश्वराय नमः

He confers salvation to the desireless doers of good on earth, for He Himself is deathless.

899. Sadhyarshi: *The God Of Gods*

ॐ साध्यर्षये नमः

Lord Shiva, as the Teacher of the Sadhyas, is the God of the gods.

113

900. Vasu-Aditya: *Vasu, The Son Of Aditi*

ॐ वसुरादित्याय नमः

He is Vasu, the Son of Aditi.

901. Vivaswan-Savita Amruta: *The Rays of The Immortal Sun*

ॐ विवस्वते – सविता अमृताय नमः

He is the Rays of the sun which bring immortality. So He is Immortal.

902. Vyasa: *The Author Of The Vedas*

ॐ व्यासाय नमः

He is the Author of the *Vedas*, the sacred *Puranas* and *Ithihasas*.

903. Sarga-Susamkshepa-Vistara: *The Maker Of Brief And Enlarged Text*

ॐ सर्गाय सुसंक्षेपाय विस्ताराय नमः

He is the Maker of brief and lengthy literature like the *Sutras* and commentaries.

904. Paryayo-Nara: *The Collective Aspect Of The Jivas*

ॐ पर्ययोनराय नमः

He is the Sum Total of the beings.

905. Ritu: *The Seasons*

ॐ ऋतवे नमः

Lord Shiva, the Controller of time, is the Seasons that are cyclic.

906. Samvatsara: *The Year*

ॐ संवत्सराय नमः

He represents the year in which each second has life, and He is felt.

907. Masa: *The Month*

ॐ मासाय नमः

He controls time and He represents the Month in which each day He is remembered.

908. Paksha: *The Fortnight*

ॐ पक्षाय नमः

He is the Fortnight when each passing moment He is worshipped.

909. Sankhyasamapana: *The New Moon And The Full Moon*

ॐ संख्यासमापनाय नमः

Lord Shiva, the Lord of time, represents both the new moon and the full moon.

910. Kala: *The Division Of Time*

ॐ कलाभ्यो नमः

He is Time, each division of which He is.

911. Kashttha: *The Minute*

ॐ काष्ठाभ्यो नमः

Lord Shiva, who is Mahakala, the Great Time, is the Minute that makes Him great.

912. Lava: *The Indication Of Small Time*

ॐ लवेभ्यो नमः

He is the Infinite Time, and every small time He indicates.

913. Matra: *Tiny Divisions Of Time*

ॐ मात्राभ्यो नमः

Every pulse, every wee division of time is manifest in Him.

914. Muhurtaha – Kshapa: *Muhurta, Day And Night*

ॐ मुहूर्ताहाः क्षपाभ्यो नमः

He manifests Himself as the Auspicious Time, Day and Night.

915. Kshana: *The Moment*

ॐ क्षणेभ्यो नमः

He is the Divine Moment when He can be realised.

916. Vishwakshetram: *The Universal Field*

ॐ विश्वक्षेत्राय नमः

He is Absolute Consciousness, the Soil on which the tree of the universe grows.

917. Prajabeejam: *The Seed For Beings*

ॐ प्रजाबीजाय नमः

He is the Unmanifested, the Consciousness enveloped by Maya, the Seed for living beings.

918. Lingam: *The Mahat*

ॐ लिंगाय नमः

He is the Mahat, the Divine Supreme, who is ever worshipful.

919. Adhya-Nirgama: *The Primal Manifestation*

ॐ आद्याय निर्गमाय नमः

He is the first Superimposition as "I", the first sprout of the universe.

920. Sat: *The Reality*

ॐ सते नमः

He is the Effects and the Reality.

921. Asat: *The Relative Reality*

ॐ असते नमः

He is the Cause and the Relative Reality.

922. Vyaktam: *The Perceptible*

ॐ व्यक्ताय नमः

He is perceptible through the senses.

923. Avyaktam: *The Unmanifest To The Senses*

ॐ अव्यक्ताय नमः

He is imperceptible, only experienced and not recognised.

924. Pita: *The Father*

ॐ पित्रे नमः

He is the Father of all.

925. Mata: *The Mother*

ॐ मात्रे नमः

He is the Mother to all beings.

926. Pitamaha: *The Grandfather*

ॐ पितामहाय नमः

He is the Divine Grandfather of all.

927. Swargadwaram: *The Door To The Heaven*

ॐ स्वर्गद्वाराय नमः

He is the Door leading to heaven through meditation.

928. Prajadwaram: *The Door To Birth*

ॐ प्रजाद्वाराय नमः

He is the Door which leads to the cycle of birth which is desire.

929. Mokshadwaram: *The Doorway To Liberation*

ॐ मोक्षद्वाराय नमः

He is the Door which leads to liberation by conquering passions.

930. Trivishttapam: *The Dharma Leading To Heaven*

ॐ त्रिविष्टपाय नमः

He is the Dharma that brings about *swarga* (heaven).

931. Nirvanam: *Liberation*

ॐ निर्वाणाय नमः

He annihilates jivahood and offers liberation to the soul.

932. Hladanam: *The World Of Brahma, The Promoter Of Delight*

ॐ हलादानाय नमः

He verily causes delight for He is pure.

933. Brahmaloka: *The World Of Brahma*

ॐ ब्रह्मलोकाय नमः

He is the Abode of Brahma called Satyaloka.

934. Paragati: *The Transcendent Goal*

ॐ परागतै नमः

He is the Supreme Goal who transcends to Brahmaloka.

935. Devasura-Vinirmata: *The Creator Of Gods And Demons*

ॐ देवासुरा विनिर्मात्रे नमः

He is the Creator of the *devas* and the *asuras*.

936. Devasuraparayana: *The Refuge Of Gods And Demons*

ॐ देवासुरपरायणाय नमः

He is the Refuge and the Supreme Goal of the gods and the demons.

937. Devasuraguru: *The Preceptor Of Gods And Demons*

ॐ देवासुरगुरवे नमः

He is the Preceptor of such beings as Brihaspati, Shukra, etc.

938. Deva: *Desirous Of Conquest*

ॐ देवाय नमः

He is the Sport and Delight, desirous of conquest.

939. Devasura-Namaskruta: *Adored By Gods And Demons*

ॐ देवासुर नमस्कृताय नमः

He is adored and worshipped by gods and demons.

940. Devasura-Mahamatra: *Superior To Gods And Demons*

ॐ देवासुर महामात्राय नमः

Lord Shiva, the Best of gods and demons, is superior to all.

941. Devasura-Ganashraya: *The King Of Gods And Demons*

ॐ श्री देवासुर गणाश्रयाय नमः

He is the King of the host of gods and demons, like Indra and Virochana.

942. Devasura-Ganadhyaksha: *Sought by Gods And Demons*

ॐ देवासुर गणाध्यक्षाय नमः

He is sought by the hosts of gods and demons.

943. Devasura-Ganagrani: *The Leader Of Gods And Demons*

ॐ देवासुर गणाग्रणै नमः

He is the Leader of the hosts of gods and demons, like Kartikeya and Kesidaitya.

944. Devadideva: *He Who Transcends The Senses*

ॐ देवादिदेवाय नमः

Lord Shiva, who controls the senses, transcends them.

945. Devarshi: *The Divine Sage*

ॐ देवर्षये नमः

He is the Divine Sage Narada who mediates for peace.

946. Devasura-Varaprada: *The Granter Of Boons To Gods And Demons*

ॐ देवासुर वरप्रदाय नमः

Lord Shiva, in the shape of Brahma and Rudra, grants boons to gods and demons.

947. Devasureshwara: *The Ruler Of Gods And Demons*

ॐ देवासुरेश्वराय नमः

The Supreme Lord Shiva rules over the gods and the demons.

948. Vishwa: *The Womb Of The Universe*

ॐ विश्वाय नमः

He is the Vast Womb in which is contained the universe.

949. Devasuramaheshwara: *The Great Lord Of Gods And Demons*

ॐ देवासुरमहेश्वराय नमः

He is the Supreme Lord ruling over gods and demons.

950. Sarvadevamaya: *Comprises All The Gods*

ॐ सर्वदेवमयाय नमः

He has Agni as His head, the sun and the moon are His eyes.

951. Achintya: *He Who Transcends Thought*

ॐ अचिन्त्याय नमः

He is the Only One to be meditated upon—He transcends thought.

952. Devatma: *The Inner Soul Of The Gods*

ॐ देवात्मने नमः

He resides in the inner soul of the gods.

953. Atmasambhava: *The Self-existent*

ॐ आत्मसंभवाय नमः

Lord Shiva, who is beyond birth and death, is Self-existent.

954. Udbhit: *Sprouts Breaking Open Ignorance*

ॐ उद्भिदे नमः

He is the Sprouts that dispel ignorance.

955. Trivikrama: *One Who Traversed The Three Worlds*

ॐ त्रिविक्रमाय नमः

He is Vamana who traversed the three worlds.

956. Vaidhya: *The Abode Of Learning*

ॐ वैद्याय नमः

He is the Abode of learning where aspirants gain proficiency.

957. Viraja: *The Stainless*

ॐ विरजाय नमः

He is stainless, unspotted—the Pure.

958. Neeraja: *Devoid Of Passion*

ॐ नीरजाय नमः

He is ever calm and composed, is devoid of the passions to elements.

959. Amara: *The Deathless*

ॐ अमराय नमः

Lord Shiva, who has no beginning or end, is deathless.

960. Eedya: *The Praiseworthy*

ॐ ईड्याय नमः

He is the most adored and cherished Deity, worthy of great praise.

961. Hastishwara: *Vayu Linga*

ॐ हस्तीश्वराय नमः

He is the Vayu Linga of Kalahasti, the reigning Deity there.

962. Vyaghra: *The Lord Of The Tiger*

ॐ व्याघ्राय नमः

He is Vyaghra, another Linga, being the Lord of the tiger.

963. Devasimha: *The Valiant Among Gods*

ॐ देवसिंहाय नमः

He is the most prowessed and valiant amongst the gods.

964. Nararshabha: *The Best Of Men*

ॐ नरर्षभाय नमः

Lord Shiva, beyond comparison, is the Best of men.

965. Vibudha: *Sharp Intellect*

ॐ विबुधाय नमः

He is full of wisdom and sharp intellect.

966. Agravara: *The First To Be Honoured In Sacrifices*

ॐ अग्रवराय नमः

He is the First to receive the sacrificial offerings.

967. Sukshma: *Incognisable*

ॐ सूक्ष्माय नमः

Lord Shiva, the Great Magician, is not easily cognisable.

968. Sarvadeva: *The Essence Of All Gods*

ॐ सर्वदेवाय नमः

He is the Sum Total of all gods, completely pervading each god.

969. Tapomaya: *Austerity Personified*

ॐ तपोमयाय नमः

The austere Lord Shiva is centred in meditation.

970. Suyukta: *Ever Attentive*

ॐ सुयुक्ताय नमः

He is extremely ready and ever attentive to listen to an aspirant's woes.

971. Shobhana: *Auspiciousness*

ॐ शोभनाय नमः

He is Pure and Auspicious.

972. Vajri: *Armed With The Vajra*

ॐ वज्रिने नमः

He is armed to the core with weapons like Vajra, the noose.

973. Prasanam Prabhava: *The Origin Of Weapons*

ॐ प्रासानाम् प्रभावाय नमः

He is the Origin from where the weapons originated.

974. Avyaya: *Unattainable By Unsteady Minds*

ॐ अव्ययाय नमः

He is attainable only through one-pointed devotion.

975. Guha: *The Hidden One*

ॐ गुहाय नमः

He is Kartikeya, the Hidden One.

976. Kanta: *The Unbounded Bliss*

ॐ कान्ताय नमः

He is Absolute Bliss.

977. Nija Sarga: *The Self-created*

ॐ निजाय सर्गाय नमः

He manifests as Self-created from whom other creations take place.

978. Pavitram: *The Protector From Death*

ॐ पवित्राय नमः

He protects one from the pangs of death that resembles a thunderbolt.

979. Sarvapavana: *The Purifier Of All*

ॐ सर्वपावनाय नमः

He purifies all, even Brahma.

980. Shrungi: *The Bull*

ॐ श्रृंगिने नमः

He is Shrungi the bull (who is the mode of transport for the Supreme Being when the Lord manifests as Shiva).

981. Shrungapriya: *Fond Of Mountain Peaks*

ॐ श्रृंगप्रियाय नमः

Lord Shiva, ever fond of mountain peaks, make them His abode.

982. Babhru: *Saturn*

ॐ बभ्रुवे नमः

Lord Shiva, the Ruler of planets, is Saturn in one of His manifestations.

983. Rajaraja: *Kubera*

ॐ राजराजाय नमः

He manifests as Kubera also.

984. Niramaya: *The Blemishless*

ॐ निरामयाय नमः

He is free from all blemishes, being absolutely Pure.

985. Abhirama: *The Producer Of Affection*

ॐ अभिरामाय नमः

He inspires gladness and affection.

986. Suragana: *The Group Of Celestials*

ॐ सुरगणाय नमः

He is the Group of celestials, residing in them.

987. Virama: *Extreme Quiescence*

ॐ विरामाय नमः

Lord Shiva, Sheer Bliss, is extremely quiescent.

988. Sarvasadhana: *The Consummation Of All Rituals*

ॐ सर्वसाधनाय नमः

He is the Consummation of such means as rituals, order of life, etc.

989. Lalataksha: *Having An Eye In His Forehead*

ॐ ललाटाक्षाय नमः

The three-eyed Lord Shiva has His third eye (of intuition) in His forehead.

990. Vishwadeva: *The Sportsman With The Universe*

ॐ विश्वदेवाय नमः

He is the Sportsman who plays with numberless worlds as with balls.

991. Harina: *The Deer*

ॐ हरिणाय नमः

He is the Deer with the soulful, gentle eyes and demeanour.

992. Brahmavarchasa: *The Spiritual Brilliance*

ॐ ब्रह्मवर्चसाय नमः

He is the spiritual radiance produced of study and meditation.

993. Sthavaranampati: *The Lord Of The Himalayas*

ॐ स्थावरणामपतये नमः

Lord Shiva, ever fond of the mountains, is the Lord of the Himalayas.

994. Niyamendriya-Vardhana: *The Conqueror Of The Senses*

ॐ नियमेन्यू – वर्धनाय नमः

He controls the senses through austere observances.

995. Siddhartha: *The Aspirant After Truth*

ॐ सिद्धार्थाय नमः

He has emancipation as His property.

996. Siddhabhutartha: *The Salvation*

ॐ सिद्धभूतार्थाय नमः

He is the Salvation, that once was His own, but was forgotten and recovered.

124

997. Achintya: *The Unthinkable*

ॐ अचिन्त्याय नमः

He is beyond the senses and difficult to be attained.

998. Satyavrata: *The Object Of All Observances*

ॐ सत्यव्रताय नमः

Lord Shiva, Truth Personified, is the Object of all meditations.

999. Shuchi: *The Pure*

ॐ शुचये नमः

He is Pure Bliss, no taints or scars.

1000. Vratadhipa: *The Granter Of The Fruits Of The Observances*

ॐ व्रताधिपाय नमः

He presides over vows and distributes fruits as justly deserved.

1001. Para: *The Supreme*

ॐ पराय नमः

He is the Supreme, the Non-dual.

1002. Brahma: *Brahman*

ॐ ब्रह्मणे नमः

He is Brahman, transcending time, space and causation.

1003. Bhaktanam-Parama-Gati: *The Highest Refuge Of The Devotees*

ॐ भक्तानां परमायै गतये नमः

Lord Shiva, unlimited by time, space, and matter, is the Highest Refuge of the devotees.

1004. Vimukta: *The Freed*

ॐ विमुक्ताय नमः

He is the Supreme Peace, unbound by any restrictions.

1005. Muktateja: *Freed Of All Limitations*

श्री मुक्ततेजसे नमः

He is the One who is free of all limitations of the body.

1006. Shriman: *Endowed With The Wealth Of Yoga*

ॐ श्रीमते नमः

Lord Shiva, free of all body limitations, attains pure Kaivalya State, which is Absolute Bliss.

1007. Shrivardhana: *The Nourisher Of The Vedas*

ॐ श्रीवर्धनाय नमः

Lord Shiva, the Author of the *Vedas*, bestows spiritual wealth on His devotees.

1008. Jagat: *The Entire Cosmos*

ॐ जगते नमः

He is the Entire cosmos enveloping and pervading all.